The eMBA Coach Playbook

The eMBA Coach Playbook

Preparing Future-Ready Leaders

Belinda H. Y. Chiu, Ed.d.

BEP

BUSINESS EXPERT PRESS

Leader in applied, concise business books

First published in 2025 by
Business Expert Press, LLC
222 East 46th Street, New York, NY 10017
www.businessexpertpress.com

ISBN-13: 978-1-63742-792-7 (paperback)
ISBN-13: 978-1-63742-793-4 (e-book)

Business Expert Press Business Career Development Collection

First edition: 2025

10 9 8 7 6 5 4 3 2 1

EU SAFETY REPRESENTATIVE
Mare Nostrum Group B.V.
Mauritskade 21D
1091 GC Amsterdam
The Netherlands
gpsr@mare-nostrum.co.uk

Description

The eMBA Coach Playbook: Preparing Future-Ready Leaders **is a toolkit for leaders, high-performers, and executive coaches. Create a positive impact through gold-standard leadership. Skillfully navigate continuous change to unlock opportunity.** Join the ranks of the future-ready, so that you can lead with a mindset of generativity and compassion.

This reusable playbook covers 52 topics chosen from over 20 years of study and practical application with thousands of clients, leaders, and MBA students and graduates:

- Module 1. Insight and awareness: wayfinding to the North Star
- Module 2. Inquiry and alignment: grounding in the face of change
- Module 3. Integration and action: communicating strategic transformation

Use this as a self-guided companion to coach yourself, your clients, and your teams on how to create innovative solutions and leave your organization—and the world—better than you found it.

Contents

Testimonials

"Both practical 'news you can use' and aspirational, The eMBA Coach Playbook *avoids the oft-repeated cliché of case study-lesson-questions-repeat and gets right down to work. I know from personal experience how these exercises can be transformational for leaders, and we are all leaders, at multiple levels in an organization."*—**Jonah Nigh, Vice President and Chief Advancement Officer, The Juilliard School**

"Every leader needs The eMBA Coach Playbook: Preparing Future-Ready Leaders! *The playbook covers 52 key themes that provide practical tools for self-reflection and, with a strong emphasis on emotional intelligence and compassionate leadership, it encourages the reader to leverage their strengths, align personal values with professional objectives, and lead with empathy. The playbook's structured yet flexible framework equips leaders to be future-ready; developing resilience, adaptability and the skills required for successful collaboration—crucial for navigating today's complex business challenges."*
—**Claire Salter, Vice President, Burberry**

*"*The eMBA Coach Playbook *provides access to valuable, field-tested content you could previously only find by sifting through stacks of books and articles on leadership, management and coaching. Dr. Chiu has done an excellent job of integrating knowledge from multiple fields of study in a way that supports rapid learning and real-world use of these insights."*—**Dr. Matthew Lippincott, cofounder and owner, Goleman Consulting Group; faculty, University of Pennsylvania and University of Toronto**

"Dr. Chiu (Belinda) distilled decades of study and hands-on experience into this practical, useful, and insightful new workbook. Whether you are a seasoned coach, aspiring new leader, or just a human being trying to find your way, these exercises will give you the tools you need to lead from within and unearth meaningful purpose in what you do."—**Casey Carpenter, President, Wheatberry Construction; U.S. Air Force Veteran (Separated at the rank of Staff Sergeant)**

"Whether you are a coach guiding your client, or a leader in an organization, Dr. Belinda Chiu's The eMBA Coach Playbook: Preparing Future Ready Leaders, *shares the best of the best evidence-based practices that will take leaders to the next level. With straightforward and actionable practices, this playbook sets the gold standard for leadership development."*—**Sarah Kivel, Founder, eiFOCUS; Author; ICF-PCC Coach; MBA candidate**

"The practicality of The eMBA Coach Playbook *comes from the bite size sessions that provide opportunities for reflection and the ability to determine actionable steps forward. Dr. Belinda Chiu has created pathways for individuals to explore what they need in their career or work well in a team environment. This playbook will be very impactful for individuals to use who are on their own learning journey and may be struggling to find a path forward, as well as for leaders to use with their teams in times of change, conflict, self-discovery, or building mode for who they are and how they want to show up for each other and their customers."*—**Jennifer Cocklin, Learning and Development, Dartmouth College**

Foreword

In today's rapidly evolving world that constantly redefines leadership, it is crucial to have the right tools to guide and develop yourself. Dr. Belinda Chiu's *The eMBA Coach Playbook: Preparing Future-Ready Leaders* offers an invaluable resource for anyone navigating the challenges of leadership development and personal growth.

I've had the privilege of knowing and working with Belinda for several years, and I've been consistently impressed by her deep understanding of human nature, her ability to inspire reflection, and her commitment to helping others become their best selves. In this playbook, she shares the actionable insights, evidence-based practices, and personal wisdom that have made her such an impactful coach and wonderful colleague.

What sets this playbook apart is its accessibility. Whether you're a seasoned coach, an emerging leader, or someone simply looking to better understand leadership dynamics, this book meets you where you are. While continuous learning is essential, finding accessible and practical tools that support both self-reflection and real-world application can be challenging. Belinda's playbook fills that gap by offering practical guidance for personal reflection, navigating change, and unlocking leadership potential.

The 52 topics covered in this playbook address the core challenges leaders face in managing themselves, their teams, and their organizations. Organized into three modules—insight and awareness, inquiry and alignment, and integration and action—the playbook takes leaders on a journey from self-awareness to strategic transformation. Designed to be revisited over time, it evolves alongside your needs, making it an ideal companion for self-coaching, working with an executive coach, or enhancing team development. Its concise sessions, reflective exercises, and actionable steps help leaders navigate complexity, make better decisions, and align their personal and professional lives in meaningful ways. No matter where you sit within an organization or what stage of your career you're in, you will encounter many of the topics and challenges addressed here.

Throughout the years, Belinda's work with countless students and professionals has helped advance their journeys to lead with purpose, authenticity, and compassion. This playbook reflects her dedication to fostering leaders who are not only successful but also impactful in the way they engage with the world. In these pages, you will find a resource to support your leadership journey—whether you're being coached, coaching others, leading teams, or striving to create positive change in your organization. This guide will empower you to meet the demands of modern leadership and thrive in a world that requires continuous adaptation.

—Richard McNulty
Executive Director, Leadership Development Programs at
Tuck School of Business
Faculty Director, Paganucci Fellows Program at Dartmouth College

Acknowledgments

It is with deep gratitude to the coaches who have and continue to coach and mentor me to greater depth and breadth of awareness and clarity. To the exquisite and excruciating editing pen of Courtney Cook Williamson, your admiration of the written word is unparalleled. Roberta Shin and Casey Carpenter, your sharp mind and strong heart as leaders inspire the possibilities of a more humanistic and compassionate approach to work. To Cathy Kim Walker, Carline DuRocher, Tsering Yangki, Patty Hines, Krishna Desai, and Rachel Kim, your wisdom and honest perspectives of what real people in a real world need are invaluable to crafting something to be of service and contribution.

To the humans who have entrusted me to support your journey as your coach, your courage, vulnerability, and wisdom to bring the best of yourself to get the best out of others and positively change the world and those who inhabit it never cease to amaze and humble.

Introduction

Why This Playbook

A playbook is a reference guide that outlines an organization's processes, practices, and strategies. In this case, instead of an organization, *you* are the focus. *The eMBA Coach Playbook: Preparing Future-Ready Leaders* is a reference toolkit for you, future-ready leaders, high-performers, and executive coaches, to codify and strategize the whys and hows of what you do. Instead of a prepared guide, *you* are the author and creator. You get to fill in the pages and chart your own path.

You might be stepping into a new leadership role or have been leading teams for decades. You might be beginning your coaching journey or have been coaching other coaches. You might be working with an executive coach or not. You're done with the old-guard systems of ego-driven power plays. You seek to reflect with curiosity, lead with wisdom, and act with purpose. You know that to be future-ready, you must "go beyond sustaining what has been, to co-create innovative solutions and leave [your] teams, organizations, and the world better than [you] found it (Chiu 2024).[1]" You want a positive impact in your careers through gold-standard leadership and skillful navigation of continuous change to unlock opportunity.

Framed within three modules: insight and awareness, inquiry and alignment, and integration and action, this playbook is meant to be jargon-free, digestible, portable, and reusable.

The Case for Coaching

At some point, you have likely navigated your career journey prescribed by a set of metrics of what it means to succeed or by being compared to others. You likely have earned accolades and have found a few (or more) things you're pretty good at, and along the way, unearthed a few growth areas. You may have surpassed many of these metrics and find yourself at a loss when there are no more tests or barometers to win. You may find yourself in uncharted waters. Or you may find yourself stuck on what you *should* be doing. Leadership can be lonely. This is why the most effective leaders have coaches.

If you are a coach, you likely have clients that have experienced all of the aforementioned. You likely search for ways to complement or accelerate your client's self-discovery process. You likely have skeptical clients who resist the reflective work between live sessions. Or you may be wondering how to continue nurturing your own development as a coach. This is why the most effective coaches have coaches.

Yet 20 years ago, there were few effective coaching resources. Coaching was often seen as a developmental last resort to address someone's bad behavior through "soft skills" (a term that is generally misunderstood. It was coined by the U.S. Army to refer to *any* skill unrelated to military machinery). While MBA programs today increasingly offer leadership courses beyond the technical aspects of finance and forecasting, there remains a gap in cultivating the essential skills of managing oneself and others.

Coaching is an opportunity to have support while reflecting with honesty and nonjudgment. The International Coach Federation describes coaching as "a thought-provoking and creative process that inspires [people] to maximize their personal and professional potential. The process of coaching often unlocks previously untapped sources of imagination, productivity and leadership.[2]"

Evidence suggests that coaching accelerates learning, improves decision making; builds leader effectiveness, self-efficacy, and self-awareness; enhances team performance; sustains organizational change; and enables leaders to optimize what they already do well.[3] The more leaders attend to their mindsets and behaviors, the more positive their impact. You have undoubtedly experienced the ripple effect leaders have.

Keep in mind that coaching is not therapy, consulting, or mentorship; this distinction is critical. Coaching is not the same as giving advice, solving problems, or trying to unpack the past. Coaching is future-focused, and you are in the driver's seat.

Coaching	Therapy	Consulting	Mentoring
Partnership	Therapist Guides	Expert-driven	Experience-driven
Future-focus	Past-focus	Problem-solving	Advice-based
Individual	Individual	Organizational	Individual
Growth	Healing	Strategic	Learning

Coaching is a powerful tool for positive transformation for the already-performing superstars and for the stars-needing-bit-of-polishing. Research suggests that leaders who bring elements of coaching see more engagement and relationships and reduced attrition.[4] While leaders' relationships with their team members are not one of a coach–coachee, leading with a coaching lens demonstrates genuine concern, helps team members align their individual values and goals to that of the organization, and effectively challenges them through active listening, powerful questions, and supportive accountability.[5]

Yet not everyone has access to effective coaching. The good news is that effective coaching skills can be taught and learned. The other good news is that in your hands now is a portable, accessible companion "coach" to support you in doing so.

The Recurring Challenges

For over 20 years of study and practical application with thousands of clients, leaders, and MBA students and graduates, I have observed a pattern of recurring challenges that people at all levels and workplaces across the globe face. These themes seem to recirculate every now and then as popular articles or titles on the proverbial bestseller's lists, like Stone, Patterson, and Heen's *Difficult Conversations*, Ury's *Getting to Yes*, or Goleman's *Emotional Intelligence*. Whether you're a C+ suite banking exec, a rising leader in pharma, an MBA student, or an executive coach, you, your teams, and your clients face similar challenges, even though they may appear within different contexts and times in your career. The advantage for you is that these themes are compiled here as a resource on

- personal and professional development (e.g., choosing a career path, finding greater purpose, balancing work and life, managing stress);
- teams and workplace dynamics (e.g., managing a new team, navigating change, transforming conflict);
- strategic transformation and change (e.g., articulating a vision, influencing others, mobilizing a team).

Grounded in a coaching philosophy based on a strengths-based, inside-out approach, this playbook distills 52 of these themes to take you on a journey of self *re*-discovery, from self-awareness to other-awareness to healthier relationships with yourself and with others.

In other words, you have all the wisdom. This playbook, your companion coach, is here to support you to (re)discover that wisdom. It aims to center you and position you to practice the *tough* skills required to work with other people to get things done.

How to Use This Playbook

(Re)discovery is a journey. It cannot only be about reading nor only about jumping into action. Following the venerated knowledge–reflection–action framework of learning, each topic has three parts:

1. EVIDENCE: jargon-free, evidence-based theory-in-practice;
2. EXPERIMENTATION: action steps; and
3. EXPLORATION: reusable reflection worksheet.

This playbook is designed to serve as your companion coach and an added resource to your already rich toolkit when coaching yourself or others. To make the most of this, let's look at some practical guidelines to diagnose what you need right now, explore optimal leadership mindsets, and prep before and process after each "session."

Playing by the Rules

There is a lot in this playbook. Don't rush to complete each worksheet in a given amount of time. Some may not apply to you at this moment, but they may in a few months, or even years. Take the time you need to pause, reflect, and practice. Give things time to breathe, test things out, see what works, see what doesn't. Then iterate and do it again.

To make the best use, here are a few general "rules" for the playbook:

- *Skip around*: find the topic that you need at the moment for yourself or your team.
- *Borrow*: take a prompt from one topic and apply it to another.

- *Bundle*: focus on a few topics together as some build on each other.
- *Take time*: don't rush; these prompts are not meant to be quickly finished in one sitting.
- *Be selective*: skip questions if you want; go back to them.
- *Get a notebook*: keep a journal of your responses.
- *Reuse*: return to the same topics over time.
- *Copy–paste*: reuse questions for your colleagues and teams.
- *Earmark*: some topics may apply now or in two years; come back when ready.
- *Keep reading*: go further if a topic interests you or you need more.
- *Be you*: answer these prompts with your "shoes-off" self—not how you think you should answer but who you are at your most authentic self.

Take some of these worksheets and give them to your team members and colleagues. Use the prompts during your 1:1s, team meetings, or team retreats. Invite your bosses to the process.

Start wherever you want. There is no grade; there are no case studies; there is no performance review. Go to what you need at this moment.

Whether this is your first or fifth time picking up this playbook, you may want to start with Module 1 (insight and awareness: wayfinding to the North Star), which takes you on the critical inward journey for grounding yourself and cultivating self-awareness. When ready, move to Module 2 (inquiry and alignment: grounding in the face of change), which supports you and your team through change and conflict. Module 3 (integration and action: communicating strategic transformation) supports you to influence, vision-set, and build team culture.

On the other hand, there may be times when things are more top of mind for you and/or your team. These are times that it may be helpful to go directly to the topic or a series of them that "play well" together.

What's on your mind:	Go to:
You don't know what you're supposed to do.	Purpose: #1, 2, 3
You want to do everything, you can't narrow it down.	
You've lost your direction and your why.	
You don't think you're good at anything.	Strengths and Motivators: #4, 6, 7, 10
You're stuck and want to get unstuck.	
You've lost your excitement for what you do.	
You're not sure how to move forward.	Goals: #12, 13, 14
You don't know where you're headed.	
You want some guidance on the next step in your career.	
You want clarity on what you stand for.	Personal Brand: #15, 16
You want greater clarity over your reputation.	
You want others to know who you are.	
You hate conflict and avoid it at all costs.	Conflict: #21, 22
You always want to win in any disagreement	
You want to handle conflict better.	
You are finding a change uncomfortable.	Change: #24, 25, 27, 28, 29, 30
You or your team seem unwilling to change.	
You need to guide your team through change.	
You don't have trust in others.	Psychological Safety: #35, 36
You don't feel safe in your team to share ideas or fail.	
Your team seems scared to speak up or make mistakes.	
Your team won't take accountability.	Team: #37, 38, 39, 40, 41, 42, 43
Your team doesn't have clarity or alignment.	
Your team has a lot of internal conflict.	
You need to influence others to follow you.	Vision: #45, 46
You have to sell an idea to others.	
You need to get everyone aligned with your ideas.	

Optimizing Your Mindset

You can optimize the effectiveness of this playbook by engaging mindfulness, emotional intelligence (EI), and compassion. Decades ago, people would scoff at the idea of mindsets and emotions in leadership. Today, research in the lab of scientific research lab and the lab of lived experience strongly point to a different reality: this blue planet's collective future depends on leaders and contributors like you who recognize that your actions and work do not exist in a bubble, but rather, a part of an inter-dependent ecosystem. People want, need, and trust leaders who have a clear moral compass, seek to create meaningful relationships, and inspire others with purpose.[6] The ever-changing world requires leaders with the mindset and skillset to stay centered, curious, and connected to how their internal worlds inform the decisions with external consequences.

The reality is when you are grounded and attuned to the present moment, you are more self- and other-aware, and importantly, with less judgment or criticism.[7] A mindful mindset is fertile ground to cultivate EI: your ability to see what's going on inside (self-awareness), so that you can manage what's happening inside (self-management), so that you can pay attention to what's going on around you (social awareness), and so that you can better relate with others (relationship management). EI is about being intelligent with and in your relationships. It is recognizing how emotions offer vital information to help you make the "rational" decisions that can impact so many others.

The last several decades of research indicate that EI is a differentiator of top-performing leaders and becomes even more important the more positional power one has.[8] EI supports leaders in their performance, decision making, and influence by building collaboration, trust, and healthy conflict.[9] It also cultivates another critical leadership mindset: compassion. Often misunderstood, especially when it comes to leadership, as being a pushover or ignoring accountability, compassion is quite the opposite. A compassionate mindset opens the door for limitless potential and performance.

In my work with MBAs and leaders, a strategic mindset is often the focus without mention of compassion. That is now changing, as the world recognizes that compassion allows for wiser and more strategic decisions, because it builds concern for the well-being of others *and* the courage to act in the face of the good, the bad, and the ugly. One study showed that 91 percent of leaders reported compassion as being very important in leadership, yet 80 percent said they don't know how but want to learn.[10] In 2024, a historic conference on Wall Street brought hundreds of the top investment banks and their leaders to discuss the role of compassion in finance. Business schools now urge the need for the integration of compassion in leadership development.[11] A compassionate mindset is no longer seen as an add-on, but a must-have. In fact, the Tibetan word for strategy, *thab-shay*, means wisdom through the method of compassion.

With market and geopolitical forces asking, "what's new? what's next?," a compassionate mindset invites you to leverage the momentum of change as the lever for generative innovation. One framework, a compassion strategy, invites you to bring greater awareness, attention, and authenticity to the kind of leader you are, aspire to be, and the world needs. Its three dimensions intersect and amplify the other (Chiu 2022a): centeredness, courage, and curiosity.[12] Centeredness enables you to stay present while investigating the past to innovate for the future.[13] Courage enables you to be honest with who you are and what matters to you, setting boundaries, and embracing healthy conflict.[14] Curiosity enables you to cultivate a deep appreciation and connection for the entirety of a system that your decisions impact.[15]

A mindset of compassion for yourself is also critical as your (re)discovery of why and how you work may open some areas of discomfort and unease. Consider how to approach learning more about yourself, including your edge areas—growth areas—with the same grace and equanimity you would want to offer your team members.

This playbook is designed with these principles to support you and those with whom you work to engage a more helpful mindset. After all, small, powerful changes can have broad ripple effects across the ecosystem.

Pre- and Postgaming

As with any development journey, it is helpful to pause and prep beforehand and to pause and process afterward. To make the most of each session, you may want to consider:

Before each session	• What prompts you to pick this playbook up today? • What are you most curious about/needing today? • What challenge are you facing?
After each session	• What made an impact on you or others? • What action are you committing to? • Who will hold you accountable?

Take time to review your explorations from each topic in your journal. Every few weeks, take a step back to observe how your mindset, behaviors, or responses to others may have shifted or not. Observe how your team members may be showing up differently or not. Share them with trusted folks who might support you to make sense of what you surface.

To be more effective and show up in a way that is meaningful and impactful for you in the workplace—and in life—takes time, honest reflection, and practice. Committing to action and holding yourself accountable is requisite for behavior change.

Importantly, don't forget that learning should be fun. Not easy, but fun. Laugh at yourself. Find the humor in the confusion. Experience the joy of a beginner's mind.

Enjoy the ride.

CHAPTER 1

Insight and Awareness

Wayfinding and Connecting to Your North Star

This module focuses on the inner work of self-awareness and purpose.

The North Star guides all forms of creatures on Earth, providing direction during the stormiest days and darkest nights and through wayward adventures and misjudged steps. Your own personal North Star gives you a reference point for your purpose. It doesn't need to be dramatic or big. It isn't a passion. It is what gets you up in the morning. It grounds you when uncertainty lies at your feet. Your North Star can evolve so it's about the journey and the choices you make along the way. By rediscovering your strengths, reframing failures, and envisioning future, you may be more able to optimize obstacles into opportunities.

These 16 worksheets support you through the process of discovery, wayfinding, visioning, energy management, self-narratives, and personal branding.

#1 Values: At the Core

Evidence

Values in action guide you in times of change. Psychologists Barb Markway and Celia Ampel noted that they are "the principles that give our lives meaning and allow us to persevere through adversity."[1] They are critical to your resilience, especially navigating an uncertain world. Your core values are things that truly matter; they make up your moral and ethical compass. They are not shiny aspirational words, but the principles by which to live and set boundaries. Being clear about your values holds you accountable to yourself and to others about what you want and how you get there.

Being aware of what you care about allows you to more clearly see what guides your thinking, behaviors, and decision making. What one word may mean to one person, may mean something entirely different to another. Behind the proverbial curtain is your own wisdom and your true self. As such, it is important to be honest and recognize that values are also just words on a piece of paper until you're tested to live by them.

Experimentation

- Pay attention when your core values are being tested.
- Be attuned to which values are mine and which ones are influenced by society/culture.
- Be purposeful in putting into action one of your values every day.

Exploration

Values prompts:

How someone can win a gold star with you...
How your personal and professional values align. How they do not.
When someone gets on your less-than-generous side, these values are being tested...
How your values are similar or different from your upbringing or culture. Which are yours. Which are ones impressed upon you by others.
You're 95. Two things you hope others will remember you for...

Values list:

reflecting on the prompts above, list five of the top values in your personal life and five in your professional life. Then distill these 10 into 5 of your core values as a whole person. Use the Sample Values for ideas.

Values in your personal life	Values in your professional life	Your Top 5 core values
How your core values show up in your daily life:		

Sample values

Acceptance	Empathy	Humility	Loyalty	Respect
Achievement	Excitement	Humor	Money	Responsibility
Adventure	Fairness	Independence	Openness	Security
Balance	Fearlessness	Integrity	Optimism	Sensitivity
Collaboration	Freedom	Intimacy	Passion	Success
Compassion	Gratitude	Knowledge	Patience	Sympathy
Confidence	Happiness	Joy	Persistence	Tolerance
Control	Harmony	Justice	Positivity	Trust
Courage	Helpfulness	Kindness	Power	Understanding
Dependable	Honesty	Love	Praise	Wealth

#2 Inflection: The Crucibles

Evidence

Leadership experts Warren Bennis and Robert Thomas define crucibles as a "transformative experience through which an individual comes to a new or an altered sense of identity."[2] These are usually unplanned experiences and often negative ones that carry with them pain and loss. But they can also be positive ones. With crucibles, you were one way before, and another way after. It can be one finite, discrete moment, or a series of moments. Some of them are obvious; others are subtle and require you to dig deeper and investigate patterns and events.

These inflection points are key to your growth. They impact how you show up to the work and for your teams. These moments test who you are and who you want to become—even if you are unaware at the moment. According to former MedTronic CEO Bill George, these are the times when you are "close to the marrow of life."[3] To understand and stay on course to your North Star, you must investigate and bring to your awareness the events and inflection points that shape who you are, how you relate to others, and what choices you make.

Experimentation

- Investigate key moments in your life and why they stand out.
- Write a story about a crucible moment and tell it to someone else.
- Practice a condensed version of a crucible moment and share it.

Exploration

Lifeline

- *Draw a horizontal line. This represents neutrality.*
- *Identify key life moments in your life—the ones above the line are positive, enriching, and joyful; the ones below are tough, painful, and trying. How far from the midline indicates the intensity of the experience.*
- *Draw a line to connect the dots—your notable life experiences.*

A lifeline is a way to visualize the peaks and valleys of your life. While you live many moments, there are those that stand out for the intensity of experience, shifts they cause, or emotional weight they carry.

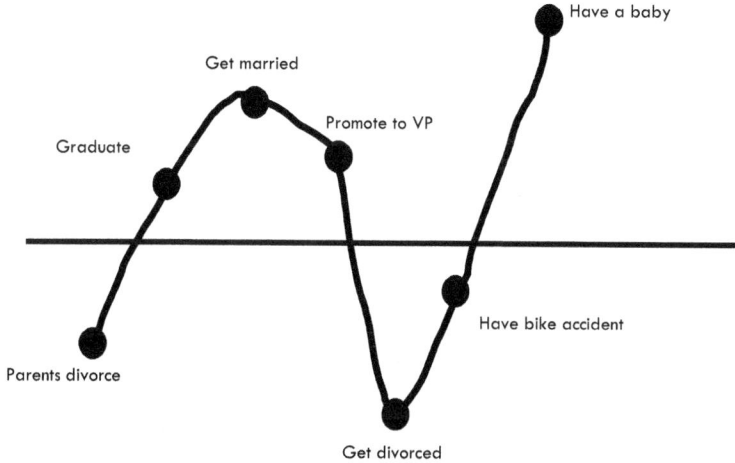

Figure 1.1 Sample lifeline

```
Your Lifeline
```

Lifeline prompts:

Observations from your lifeline…
Themes, patterns, and trends that you notice…
How these moments changed your outlook/perspective/behavior…
How these moments impact you now…

Crucible prompts:

Two to three crucible moments in your life/career you want to call attention to…
How these have shaped who you are today and what you stand for (your North Star)…

#3 Purpose: The Why

Evidence

While most leaders say purpose positively impacts employee satisfaction and productivity, innovation and transformation, and customer loyalty,[4] less than half say purpose informs their strategic and operational decision making, and fewer than 20 percent of leaders have a clear sense of their own purpose.[5] Grounded in your values and identity, purpose is not about what or how you do what you do, but *why* you do what you do. Purpose gives you meaning. Simon Sinek famously mapped the why-how-what framework to the brain's wiring, which starts with the universal need for safety, connection, and belonging. He emphasized that knowing your *why* is critical to your own sense of fulfillment and meaning, as well as inspiring others to action.[6]

Purpose allows you to take a more holistic and long-term time horizon perspective, rather than a short-term rationale for a tactical execution. Purpose is not the same as passion; it is what keeps you grounded. It gives meaning to the multiple reasons you give yourself to do or not do, creating the conditions for growth.

Experimentation

- Write a purpose statement in one or two sentences—like a newspaper headline.
- Identify one action to start today to get closer to the mission.
- Ask a trusted friend or colleague their reactions to the headline.

Exploration

Purpose prompts:
- *imagine that you are a company (you as an entity).*
- *consider what makes you unique*
- *consider what is success*
- *clonsider your short- and long-term vision and strategy*

Mini-example: Motto—be the joy. Mission—to help others find their joy so they can have the most positive impact on others and the world. Unique selling proposition (USP)—blend of research and practice, of seriousness and humor, of compassion and directness. Well-lived life— full of adventure, friends, and family, actively doing more good than not in the world, actively helping those who need support. One-year strategy—learn a new skill, get a certification or degree. Ten-year vision—run forest tea house, rescue wildlife and animals from climate disasters.

Your motto (what you're about—a tagline)...	Your mission (why you do what you do)...
Your USP: three things that make you different from your peers and colleagues (what makes you, you)...	How you define a life well-lived (how you want to live)...
Your one-year strategy to achieve your mission (how you want to behave)...	Your 10-year vision (or two, three, five-year—how you want to grow)...

#4 Flow: Energizers and Deflators

Evidence

Recognizing the conditions that enable you to be in what psychologist Mihaly Cziksentmihalyi calls *optimal experience* leads to better alignment, purpose, and enjoyment.[7] This sense of *flow* is a cognitive state where you are fully immersed in an activity, fully present and absorbed in an activity, and time seems to dissipate. When you're in a state of flow, your creativity, productivity, and psychological well-being increase.[8] You are highly focused on the task at hand and are clear-eyed on your goal; you are fully present to the experience rather than caught in ruminative, self-critical worry; and you are challenged appropriately for the level of skill you have.

George Mumford, whose mindfulness teachings helped the Chicago Bulls and L.A. Lakers win back-to-back championships, notes that it isn't just about the experience itself, but about the conditions to be *flow ready*.[9] While you cannot avoid all uncomfortable or energy-depleting activities, being flow ready requires moment-by-moment awareness to identify and embrace more of the conditions where you thrive. Understanding what energizes you—and what doesn't—helps you to discover more moments of flow.

Experimentation

1. Track your energy-driving and energy-depleting activities a day.
2. Take one action to reduce one of your energy-depleting activities a day.
3. Commit to doing one energy-driving activity a day.

Exploration

Energizer prompts:

You can talk all day about…	You love the work when you…
Time flies when you…	You resist the work when you…
Time crawls when you…	You leave work energized when…
	You leave work de-energized when…
Even if you didn't get paid, you would…	What brings you joy…

Energizer list:

reflecting on the previous prompts, list your top energizers and deflators. Consider opportunities to dial them up or down.

Your energizers	Your deflators

Flow prompts:

Opportunities to explore your energizers…	Ways you can reduce your deflators…
You are in flow when…	

#5 Prioritization: Bento Box of Attention

Evidence

One study showed that 65 percent of meetings are considered interruptions, 71 percent are considered unproductive, and 64 percent detract from important thinking time.[10] With everything seeming like it is a priority, it seems almost impossible to figure out where to put your attention. The pressure to do it all at once and multitask is fierce, as technology adds to the speed and demand of turnaround.[11] But your brain is not designed to constantly switch from task to task. Anytime you switch tasks, there is a *switch cost*, which is a reduction in speed and performance.[12]

While you cannot change time, you can work smarter with what you have. Rather than default to your tendency to dive into juggling everything to avoid overwhelm, take time and identify which tasks are the most critical to reach your North Star goal, which tasks require a lot of time and attention, and which ones may be deferred to a later date (or even removed). This is an ongoing, iterative process, as things shift, and you need to remain agile to adjust accordingly.

Experimentation

1. Make a commitment to your ideal bento box.
2. Ask someone for support to keep yourself accountable.
3. Share your bento box with others.

Exploration

Bento box of attention:

- *imagine your time being like a bento box, which has limitations to how much it can hold.*
- *draw the compartments that represent the size of how your attention and energy are currently divided in your current box (take out 'First').*
- *draw your ideal time structure in your aspirational box (take out 'Then').*

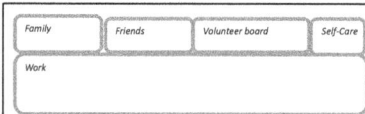

| Family | Friends | Volunteer board | Self-Care |
| Work | | | |

Figure 1.2 Sample current box of attention

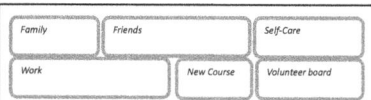

| Family | Friends | | Self-Care |
| Work | | New Course | Volunteer board |

Figure 1.3 Sample aspirational box of attention

Your current box of attention

Your aspirational box of attention

#6 Motivators: Drive Style

Evidence

Tapping into your motivation gives you a sense of purpose and agency, without which you become less persistent in the face of challenge.[13] Motivational science affirms that you crave growth and process. Intrinsic motivation may be competence-based (learning), challenge-based (accomplishment), control-based (agency), or attitudes-based (belief). Extrinsic motivation may be reward- or fear-based, achievement-based (goal), power-based (control), or affiliation-based (belonging).[14]

Motivation can also give you a better awareness of why you behave in certain ways. For some of you, it is about getting the job done quickly; for others, it is about getting it done well. One way is no better than another. Awareness allows you to better know why you are particular about some things and not so much about others. Recognizing what motivates others helps you to better understand the intentions behind their behaviors, rather than make assumptions. Connecting with what drives other people helps you be more influential and increases the chances of getting buy-in.

Experimentation

1. Reflect on how your behaviors are driven by your motivational style.
2. Observe what others' motivational styles might be based on their behavior.
3. Engage with someone by grounding in motivational styles, rather than behavior.

Exploration

Motivation questionnaire:
based on the Strength Deployment Inventory,[15] *this questionnaire serves as an indicator, not a definitive assessment.*

Circle your preference (don't overthink)	A	B
1	You feel most satisfied when you	Get things done	Get things right
2	You don't like things that are	Done improperly	Boring

3	You are drawn to things that	Are new and different	Help others
4	You tend to	Plan things out	Start immediately
5	You make decisions based on	People and relationships	Facts and evidence
6	Projects should	Achieve set goals	Generate possibilities
7	Conflicts are	More harmful to teams	More helpful to teams
8	Decisions should be made	Deliberately	Collaboratively
9	Work should	Be in service to others	Change status quo
10	You would rather be known for being	Innovative	Accurate

Pick the quote that speaks to you. Circle the letter (don't overthink)		
11	Alone we can do so little; together we can do so much ~Helen Keller	A
	Anything worth doing, is worth doing right ~Hunter Thompson	B
	If you wait for perfect conditions, you will never get anything done ~Ecclesiastes	C
	Great minds discuss ideas; average minds discuss events; small minds discuss people ~Eleanor Roosevelt	D

Motivation scoring:

circle your answers from the previous table. Count the number of boxes in each row you circled. Put the number by each row in "Score" and corresponding "Code."

						Score	Code
1A	4B	5B	6A	7B	11C		G
1B	2A	4A	8A	10B	11B		P
3B	5A	7A	8B	9A	11A		R
2B	3A	6B	9B	10A	11D		I

Motivation styles:

based on your highest (or two highest) scores by "Code," review which motivational style you may prefer.

	G Goal	P Process	R Relationships	I Idea
Motivated by:	Challenge	Accuracy	Networking	Ideas
Fulfilled by:	Getting things done	Doing things well	Working with people	Being open to possibilities
Done well:	Decisive	Rigorous	Sincere	Enthusiastic
Overdone:	Aggressive	Perfectionist	Overprotective	Short attention

#7 Strengths: Flexing You

Evidence

With 25 million data points and almost 12K teams, Gallup found that teams with 90 percent of their employees knowing their strengths were more engaged.[16] Those who are aware of and utilize their strengths see a positive impact on performance metrics like productivity, profitability, and psychological well-being.[17] A strengths-based approach places the individual as the agent of change. Rather than having a deficit mindset, centering your positive abilities enables you to address your areas of growth.

Strengths sit at the intersection of your natural preferences of thought, feeling, and behavior, and what you spend time developing, which means that strengths aren't just things you are good at. You may share a strength with someone else, but how it plays out is influenced by context and the interplay with your other strengths. While others see your strengths as what makes you unique, you often take them for granted because they come to you with more ease, and when things seem easy, it can feel like you aren't working. Self-awareness is critical to understanding your unique constellation of strengths and how best to utilize them. Otherwise, you may overplay or misuse them if you are unaware of how they impact others.[18] Reflecting on and putting your strengths into practice helps you to have a more favorable self-view[19] and increase your happiness.[20]

Experimentation

1. Identify three tasks or activities to build on your strengths.
2. One relationship you want to cultivate to build on your strengths.
3. Identify one opportunity to explore to build on your strengths.

Exploration

Strength prompts:

One day in the last three months you really enjoyed what you were doing and who you were with, you were…
Your colleagues would say your strengths are…

You feel knowledgeable and comfortable speaking about/doing…
The activities and tasks that come most easily and naturally for you are…

When you are energized, you use your strengths of…	A strength you may be overdoing is…
What you do well naturally that you don't always think about as strengths is…	A strength you may be underutilizing is…
Strengths you have put time into developing even though they are not particularly natural are…	What you do well that is not particularly energizing is…

Strength list:
reflecting on the previous prompts, list your top five core strengths.

Your top five core strengths…

Using strengths:
write each of your top five strengths. Reflect on how each strength helps you to:

	Strength 1	Strength 2	Strength 3	Strength 4	Strength 5
Influence action					
Influence others					
Reach my goals					
Manage conflict					
Navigate change					
Complement other people's strengths					

#8 Stories: Reframing Self-Narratives

Evidence

You are a storyteller. You not only tell stories to others, but you tell stories about yourself to yourself. The filters through which you see and make sense of the world shape your cognitive understanding, emotional responses, and behaviors. Because your brain is wired to see the negative in any situation because of an evolutionary safety net, the unhelpful stories often become the loudest. If you don't investigate these stories, you can take these stories as the immutable truth. These stories often lead you to question your own competency and adequacy. You may buy into the story that you are not worthy if you don't do everything right, do it all, do it perfectly, or do it yourself. At least 70 percent of people experience this sense of inadequacy at some point,[21] which often leads to unhelpful and unsubstantiated self-criticism. This voice can come in the form of your inner critic.

On the other hand, it is important not to completely ignore criticism that could be useful for your growth. If you choose to get curious about these stories and investigate what's behind them, you may be able to better discern any useful and constructive lessons and reframe the limiting self-narratives. This voice can come in the form of your inner sage. Those who leverage their inner sage and transform constructive feedback show higher levels of resilience and well-being.[22]

Experimentation

1. Observe when unhelpful narratives pop up and pause to interrupt.
2. Identify helpful habits and patterns.
3. Discern when your inner sage speaks and when your inner critic speaks.

Exploration

Recurring unhelpful story prompts:

A recurring theme or pattern that negatively impacts you…	
The story you tell yourself based on this theme or pattern…	
Key points of this story…	When does this story show up…
What it says about you…	How it impacts your thinking…
How it impacts your emotional responses…	How it impacts your behavior…

Reframing story prompts:

An alternative version of the unhelpful story…	
Key points of this story…	When might this story be useful…
What it says about you…	How it would impact your thinking…
How it would impact your emotional response…	How it would impact your behavior…
How you will interrupt your current narrative…	
How you will communicate this reframing to others…	

#9 Resilience: Failing Forward

Evidence

Resilience isn't something you are born with; it is influenced by your natural disposition and external environments, including positive experiences and supportive relationships.[23] While resilience is often explained as bouncing back from a setback or failure,[24] it is about bouncing forward. Rarely can you go back to what was. But you can get stronger. Indeed, failure is an indicator that you have challenged yourself. Without failure, you do not learn.

While some companies frown upon failure; others reward failure. Some organizations even recognize those who take risks, even if they fail, with the *Penguin Award* in honor of the first penguin bold enough to dive into a cold sea full of predators. Yet even if you may feel safe to fail in one environment, there are others where you may not feel that way. In those moments, your ability to positively respond in the face of adversity becomes paramount. Resilience enables you to reflect on your failures, not berate yourself. Cognitively, it makes sense; believing it is another story. Reminding yourself that failure is neither a permanent nor universal statement of who you are, your worth, or your competence builds your resilience. In turn, resilience positively impacts your well-being, performance, and engagement.[25]

Experimentation

1. Identify one opportunity to embrace failure.
2. Share your failures with your team.
3. Recognize and honor when someone else takes a risk and fails.

Exploration

Lessons from failure prompts:

A situation where you failed or didn't achieve what you had hoped…	
Your role/contribution to this failure…	What was happening outside your control…
What was within your control…	What went well with this situation…
What you can do better the next time…	What this experience says about your resilience…
Three lessons to take away…	Why you're grateful for this experience…

#10 Flourish: The Sum of Joys

Evidence

Flourishing is identifiable with a sense of *eudaimonia*, during which you are living the best version of yourself,[26] which, in turn, can lead to higher performance and well-being.[27] Eudaimonia is the ongoing state of living in alignment with your values and "fulfilling one's virtuous potential and living as one was inherently intended to live."[28] Flourishing is not a temporal state of happiness. Even after a big positive experience, such as winning the lottery,[29] your state of happiness returns to a set point, known as *hedonic adaptation*.[30] Flourishing is a sustained state of optimal well-being made up of life's big, ecstatic highs and small, understated joys. It involves all aspects of life and allows for vitality and fulfillment.

Paying constant attention to the small things is critical for eudaimonic well-being and a life of flourishing. It can be increased by practicing *ikigai*, a Japanese term that has been often misinterpreted in mainstream media as purpose. While there is no direct translation for ikigai, it refers to a sense that life is worth living and is both a target and a state of mind. It is about engaging in the little things, even the most mundane experiences, an accumulation of small joys that make life worth living.[31] Being more aware of the conditions that may promote these moments increase your opportunity to flourish.

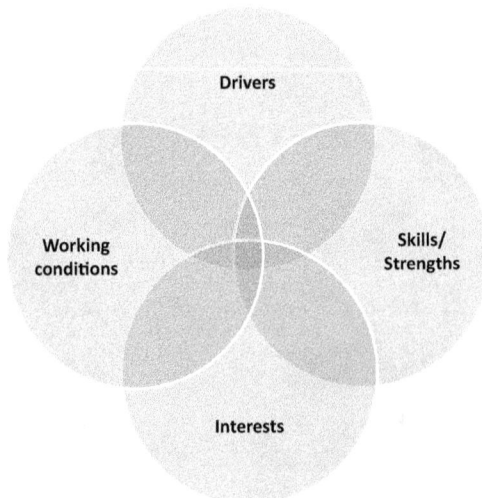

Figure 1.4 Flourish

Experimentation

1. Commit to one small act of joy a day for you.
2. Ask what brings a team member joy.
3. Write down a word of gratitude before bed.

Exploration

Flourish prompts:

	You're stressed. You feel anxious.	You're relaxed. You feel peaceful.
What you are doing…		
Who you are with…		
What values show up (or not)…		

You look forward every day to…
The small things that make you smile every day are…
You are motivated by…
Tasks or activities that bring the best out of you…
You are energized and excited by…
Environments you do your best in look like this, sound like this, feel like this…
20 years from now, you want to…

#11 Energy: Rhythm Ration

Evidence

Your circadian rhythm is the natural cycle of your body's internal functions and processes. Research on this topic even earned three scientists a Nobel Prize. The circadian rhythm for most humans ranges from 20 to 28 hours, during which your energies wax and wane. As much as you may try to fight it, your genes determine your chronotype—about 15 percent of the population would prefer to wake up before dawn, about 15 percent go to bed well after the moon rises, and the rest somewhere in between if it weren't for alarm clocks and work.[32]

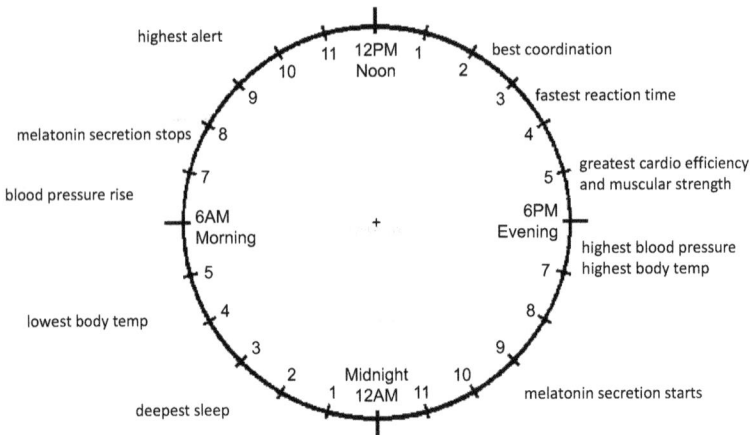

Figure 1.5 Circadian rhythms

While you can't change everyone's schedules, you can more intentional about matching your work to your natural energies (e.g., mental energy in morning = writing in the morning). Your daily rhythms move through three key cycles that can align to a type of work: peak (highest vigilance—analytical work), trough (fatigue—administrative work), and recovery (mood recovers—creative work).[33] You may have several cycles or one long one throughout the day. When you align your tasks more to energy, you perform better and more efficiently—and feel better. As they say, work smarter, not harder.

Experimentation

1. Map your rhythms across your peaks and troughs across different types of energies: physical (active), mental (clarity), and emotional (connect with others, resilience).
2. Adjust one task to your natural rhythm.
3. Pay attention to others' rhythms and align tasks together to optimize both.

Exploration

Energy quotient prompts:
reflect on your natural rhythms in general. Consider the percentage of average energy you have by the hour—where are your peaks, troughs, and recovery? For more nuance, you can draw a different one for your physical, emotional, and mental space. It can be helpful to observe yourself over the course of a week.

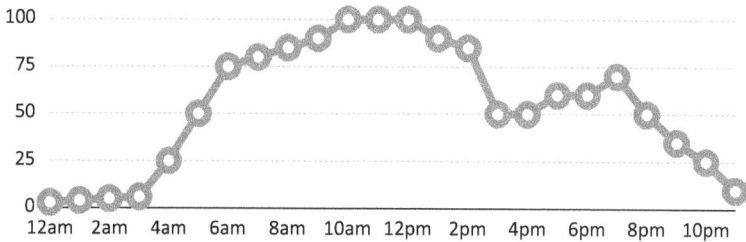

Figure 1.6 Sample energy quotient

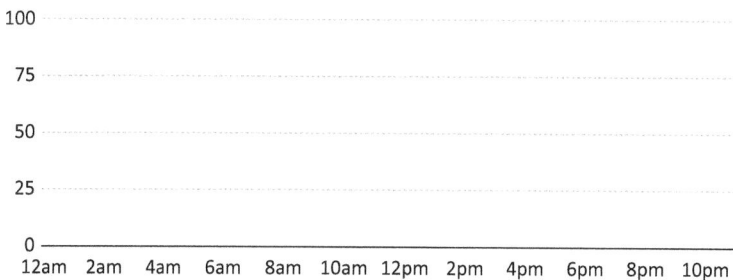

Figure 1.7 Your energy quotient

Task prompts:

identify your most common daily tasks, what level of natural energy you have during that time, and what level and type of energy you need to complete them most effectively and efficiently. Reflecting on your energy quotient map, observe what might be a more ideal time of day to do the task.

Task	Current time you usually do this task	Your natural level of energy during this time of day	Level of energy needed for the task (high/ medium/low)	Type of energy needed for the task (physical/ mental/ emotional)	Ideal time of day for the task based on your natural energy

#12 Metaphor: Picture This

Evidence

Metaphors transfer meaning from one thing to another and "build a bridge from the known to the unknown."[34] By connecting something abstract to a recognizable image or form, metaphors stimulate memory processes in the brain. As a leader, using metaphors can help you to make sense of your own value systems, assumptions, and behaviors. Many people tend to default to words, yet research shows that using imaginative metaphors heightens self-awareness and a renewed sense of empowerment and agency.[35] Doing so is critical to gaining insight, sensemaking, processing, and stimulating action.[36]

Using visual representations supports the self-discovery process. Such metaphors activate your insula, the part of the brain associated with emotion, empathy, and sensory processing. Metaphors and visual imagery clarify what and how you want to convey your ideas and who you are to others and to do so in a way that is memorable, accessible, and compelling. Inviting your brain to access parts of your thoughts and emotions other than the world of words you likely spend most of your time in can surface latent ideas and insights.

Experimentation

1. Share your metaphor with others.
2. Invite your team members to share their metaphors.
3. Practice conveying and communicating ideas nonverbally.

Exploration

Metaphor:

without using words or letters, draw an image or metaphor that reflects your aspiration or vision for how you want to show up for others, as a leader, or for a project.

Metaphor prompts:

Meaning or takeaway from this metaphor—what this image say about you? Your vision...
To whom you want to share this metaphore. What you want them to understand...

#13 Goals: Future Flourish

Evidence

New Year's goals generally start out hopeful. Yet within one week, 23 percent of individuals give up, and by two years, the percentage that abandons their well-intentioned goals increases to 81 percent.[37] There are two dimensions that underscore behavioral change: motivation (the will) and the cognitive (the way).[38] Whereas the way is connected to your brain's executive function, the why connects to your brain's reward systems. When you don't know one or the other, achieving goals becomes far more difficult.

Not only do you need to be ready for change, but you also need to have a sense of self-efficacy and the skills to make the change. The level of intensity, skill needed, and motivation depends on the type of goal. Goals that seek to add something, rather than avoid something, are more successful.[39] Rather than just stating a goal and hoping for the best, exploring what the future goal might look like, sound like, and feel like to us with a level of specificity may shed light on what might support you and what might get in the way.

Experimentation

1. Share your two-year goal with one person.
2. Actively work to address a skill gap in your way of getting to this goal.
3. Ask one person to hold you accountable.

Exploration

Future flourish prompts:

A time you flourished at work…
The part of you that was flourishing…
What you were doing and feeling…
What you learned from the experience…

Visualize yourself in two years…
What is different…
What is the same…
What you are doing/feeling more of…
What you are doing/feeling less of…
What others are saying about you…

What you hope to do/achieve in two years…
Why you are motivated to do this…
What skills/resources you need to help…
What might get in the way and what you will do to mitigate these obstacles…

#14 Visioning: Predicting You

Evidence

According to Regina Pally, when you envision something, your predictive brain unconsciously endeavors to help you reach that vision—even if it doesn't look exactly like how you first imagined—to sync with an idealized image of yourself.[40] You set into motion what you hope to see. Visualization is a powerful tool to leverage your brain's predictive orientation. Humans are naturally motivated to achieve, which promotes a sense of self-efficiency and self-mastery. Athletes and musicians often use visualization to prepare themselves by imagining moving their bodies in the way they envision. Imagining the action trains their muscles as if they were moving them.[41]

Research shows a strong correlation between goal setting, self-esteem, confidence, and autonomy.[42] From a neurobiological perspective, goal setting stimulates your medial prefrontal cortex into action, to consider what you need to get to the goal and how to go about it. Your motivation increases when you are inspired, which an aspiration vision helps to do. A vision is a picture of a future that is better than today. This is different from a mission or values, the former being a statement of why you are doing something and the latter articulating how you behave as you enact your mission to realize your vision.

Experimentation

1. Reflect on one detail that you want to start putting into action today.
2. Write a version with a different timeline—one year from now, five years from now.
3. Consider one current block in the way of your vision and one action to mitigate it.

Exploration

Vision prompt:
imagine yourself three years from now, you are content, fulfilled, and living the best version of yourself. What are you doing (less about a role/title)? Who are you with? What are the qualities of your relationships? What does your world look like? Feel like? Set a timer and just write. Add details; be specific. When you're done, what words or phrases pop out to you?

#15 Aspiration: Unique Tagline

Evidence

A tagline summarizes what is unique about you and articulates your North Star. It gives clarity when you make difficult decisions and whether a choice aligns with your tagline. Integrity and consistency are key leadership qualities.[43] After all, others look to see whether your decisions or actions align with who you say you are. Leaders who can articulate their why can better inspire, get buy-in to their vision, and motivate them towards action. This articulation helps others know what they're getting when they work with or follow you.

The simpler the message, the more effective. Indeed, taglines are most compelling when they have clarity, creativity, and credibility to build attention, memorability, and affinity.[44] A succinct, compelling, memorable, and unique statement should reflect who you are and why you do what you do.

Experimentation

1. Get feedback on your tagline.
2. Identify one place where you will communicate your tagline.
3. Draw an image that would reflect your tagline.

Exploration

Tagline prompts:
there is no one right way to write a tagline. Some best practices include being authentic, action-oriented, concise, unique, credible, relatable, and hopeful.

Mini examples:

I help you organize your time so you can organize your life.
I teach businesses to communicate their values to the world.
Translating research to everyday use.

In one or two brief sentences, your leadership "tagline" or aspirational headline…
What it says about your natural strengths…
What it says about your values that are unique you…
What emotions you want your tagline to be associated with…
What is unique about your tagline…
What others should expect from you based on this tagline…
What you want others to remember about you…
What opportunities you say yes to that support your tagline…
What opportunities you will say no to that do not align with your tagline…

#16 Brand: The M.A.G.I.C. of Personal Branding

Evidence

While branding is a integral to the marketing industry, research on personal branding is still in its infancy. One meta-study found five attributes of personal branding: it is strategically directed, designed to leave a positive impression on others, declares a promise of some benefit, is created with individual agency, and involves narrative and imagery.[45] Just as a product brand speaks to its unique selling proposition (USP), your personal brand also needs to reflect your unique constellation of why you do what you do (your purpose), how you do what you do (your values), what your goals are (your intention), what you bring to the table (your skills), and what makes you credible (your track record).

Your personal brand precedes you. It is your reputation, made up of your beliefs, attitudes, behaviors, and expectations others have of you.[46] Your brand is your own *M.A.G.I.C.*: who you are (*Me*), what you have done (*Accomplishments*), what you want (*Goals*), what you are known for (*Image*), and what credibility you bring (*Credentials*). A brand must feel authentic to you and others, relatable and understandable, compelling and inspiring, and uniquely identifiable as you. Being proactive about your personal brand means having more agency over your reputation and ability to inspire and engage others.

Experimentation

1. Share your M.A.G.I.C. Personal Brand with someone.
2. Consider how you would tailor my brand to my audience.
3. Draw an image to accompany your personal brand.

Exploration

M.A.G.I.C. prompts:
reflect on the five components of the M.A.G.I.C. of Personal Branding including me (who I am), accomplishments (what I've done), goals (my intention), image (what I want to be known for), credentials (why I'm the right person). Write a brief statement for each.

Mini example:

I am a wizard known for my courage and loyalty. I have saved my school from destruction, earned three advanced degrees, and one championship....

Me prompts:

Who you are...	How others see you...
What you currently do...	What makes you different...
Me (in brief)...	

Accomplishments prompts:

Three results you have achieved (be specific)...	Value and impact you have had on others...
Three skills you have demonstrated ...	How these skills translate to other areas...
Accomplishments (in brief)...	

Goals prompts:

What you hope to achieve/what your target...	Why this is important...
What is your desired impact...	What success looks likes...
Goals (in brief)...	

Image prompts:

Your presence can be described as...	What you want others to think/feel/do about you...
Others would describe your style as...	What you want to be known for...
Image (in brief)...	

Credentials prompts:

Professional affiliations ...	Civic or volunteer affiliations...
Academic or professional certifications...	Recognitions and awards...
Publications and thought leadership...	Speaking opportunities...
Credentials (in brief)...	

M.A.G.I.C.: reflecting on the prompts above, write a more complete statement about your brand.

Your three-minute M.A.G.I.C. version	Your one-minute M.A.G.I.C. version

CHAPTER 2

Inquiry and Alignment

Grounding in the Face of Change

This module focuses on grounding yourself to navigate conflict and change.

Times of upheaval and ambiguity can leave you feeling unmoored and more susceptible to conflict. Embracing and transforming conflict invites more honest and open dialogue to ensure alignment and welcome other perspectives to stay on course toward the North Star. It is also important to ensure that you have a support system to ground you through big and small transitions. Cultivating your resilience builds your agility to pivot and stay nimble. Agility also trains you to be attuned to your attention appropriately to the long-term and the short-term, which in turn help you to discern a more effective and wiser course of action.

These 18 worksheets support you through the process of alignment, change with agility, conflict transformation, and compassionate candor.

#17 Alignment: You'Sync

Evidence

Research shows that when you feel more aligned with your team and organization, you are more committed and engaged. Alignment gives you and your team members greater clarity and autonomy to play your respective roles in achieving shared goals.[1] It builds trust and engagement. Engagement can be seen from the cognitive (conceptual shared purpose), emotional (emotive bond), and behavioral (investment and intention to act) lenses, which impact individual performance.[2] By tuning into how your values affect your team, you are more effective and are more likely to inspire commitment, performance, and well-being.

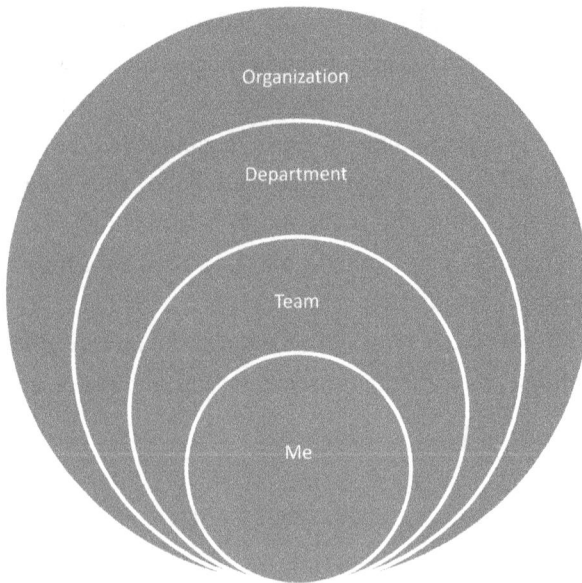

Figure 2.1 Alignment

Alignment doesn't mean that you always agree; it means that you are in sync with your team and organization's shared set of values, purpose, and goals. This becomes even more important during times of change, whether it is a personal transition or organizational or policy changes that may impact your work.

Experimentation

1. Write down the time and date to speak with your supervisor about an opportunity.
2. Discuss individual mission and values with team members to find alignment.
3. Seek out one way to ground yourself in your mission and values in the face of change.

Exploration

Alignment prompts:

Organization's mission; your organization's values...
Department's mission; your department's values...
Team's mission; your team's values...
Your mission; your values...
Ways your mission and values align with your team, department, and organization...
Ways your daily work align with you, your team, department, and organization...
One way to commit to your mission and values, especially through change...

Opportunities prompts:

Opportunities that align with your mission and values that already exist in your current role	Opportunities that align with your mission and values that you could explore in your department outside your current role
Opportunities that align with your mission and values that you could explore outside your organization	Opportunities that align with your mission and values that you could explore outside your department at your organization

#18 Capabilities: Optimizing Skills

Evidence

Capabilities are simply the things you can do. Unlike strengths, which includes your natural preferences, capabilities are skills you have spent time developing and honing. You may have capabilities you love to flex and others you don't have great affinity for. Knowing your capabilities is one thing; knowing how to optimize them to align with and contribute to a team in your unique way is another. Particularly through change, personal or otherwise, creating a compelling case about what you're good at builds others' belief in us and our ability to influence them.[3] Being intentional about how your capabilities fit can help you understand how your team can get the best out of you, and you to be more indispensable to them.

You also must communicate your contributions to demonstrate your unique impact. Doing so helps you to build greater trust and stronger relationships. It allows you and the other person to have more candid recognition of what each brings to the table without making assumptions or making misjudgments about your behavior and intention. More open dialogue about your capabilities allows others more insight into our perspectives, points of view, and capabilities.

Experimentation

1. Identify one audience you want to communicate to about your capabilities.
2. Share your unique contributions to increase your influence with your team.
3. Ask each team member to share their unique contributions with each other.

Exploration

Capabilities prompts:
write down the things you're skilled and capable at, including those things you often take for granted. Then note on a high–medium–low scale: how unique it is to your current team/project, how important it is to your goal/ team/project, how beneficial it is for your target audience (e.g., senior leadership and cross-functional peers), how much in demand it is by others, how much growth potential it has for you (e.g., room to keep learning), and how much you enjoy it.

Capability	Unique	Importance	Audience	Demand	Growth	Enjoyment
	H/M/L	H/M/L	H/M/L	H/M/L	H/M/L	H/M/L

Which capabilities you are overplaying that aren't as aligned with your or the team's need…
Which capabilities you are underplaying that are needed…

#19 Decisions: Calculating Risk

Evidence

When you encounter a crossroads, it is easy to get stuck. Maybe it is between two jobs; maybe it is about quitting one. Tough decisions are often tough because there are positives to both (or all) choices. Or the opposite. Your fear of making the wrong choice can be paralyzing. When you're fearful, you become more anxious. When you're more anxious, you are more likely to make decisions that lead you to take higher, more unwise risks.[4]

Yet rather than trying to shy away from tough decisions, reminding yourself that you "have the power to create reasons for [yourself] to become the distinctive people that [you] are"[5] can help you be more intentional about cost-benefit analysis. You also need to check your own biases that may impact such an analysis, such as confirmation bias (what we already believe in), sunk-cost fallacy (overemphasis on loss), and expedience (quick action). Experiencing agency in your decision making allows you to be more adept at calculating risk.

Experimentation

1. Set a deadline for you to make this decision.
2. Notice what your body is trying to tell about this decision.
3. Ask yourself: which choice are you trying to avoid?

Exploration

Opportunity and risk prompts:
list the opportunities you want to evaluate the pros and risks for. Then rate based on high–medium–low: operational complexity (difficulty of process and management), ease of implementation, fit with your goals, resource costs, market demand, and potential profit. Rate each according to the corresponding score (1 to 3). Total each row. The higher the score, the more benefit the opportunity may offer that outweighs the risks.

Opportunity:						
Operational complexity	Ease of implementation	Fit with goal	Costs	Market demand	Potential profit	Score
H = 1 M = 2 L = 3	H=3 M=2 L=1	H = 1 M = 2 L = 3	H = 1 M = 2 L = 3	H=3 M=2 L=1	H=3 M=2 L=1	

Opportunity:						
Operational complexity	Ease of implementation	Fit with goal	Costs	Market demand	Potential profit	Score
H = 1 M = 2 L = 3	H=3 M=2 L=1	H = 1 M = 2 L = 3	H = 1 M = 2 L = 3	H=3 M=2 L=1	H=3 M=2 L=1	

Opportunity:						
Operational complexity	Ease of implementation	Fit with goal	Costs	Market demand	Potential profit	Score
H = 1 M = 2 L = 3	H=3 M=2 L=1	H = 1 M = 2 L = 3	H = 1 M = 2 L = 3	H=3 M=2 L=1	H=3 M=2 L=1	

Which factors are more or less critical at this moment…
What other factors do you need to consider…
How might existing biases impact your decision making…
Which opportunities offer more benefit than risk…

#20 Network: Personal Board of Advisors

Evidence

According to Rob Cross, a strong network of people boosts your resilience.[6] A strong network offers notable benefits, including helping you to: stay true to our purpose, maintain perspective; see a path forward, self-advocate, understand the bigger picture, prioritize, manage emotions, and find humor. Of course, no one person can fulfill all your needs.[7] Those you count on should represent a diversity of skills. Just as a company has a range of skills on their board, you too can with your own personal board of advisors. Your personal board isn't just made up of individuals who tell you what you want to hear nor are they necessarily even within your field or industry. They are individuals who have your best interest.[8]

Your personal board of advisors is not your cadre of job hunters; they help you look at things differently, challenge you, encourage you, and connect you to a broader network. It is the expanded network of your immediate circle of contacts that demonstrates the greatest capacity to be impactful.[9] You need to be clear with those on your board why you have included them and how supporting you aligns with their motivation for a mutually beneficial, sustained relationship. It must be a bidirectional personal investment.

Experimentation

1. Reach out to each member of your board to ask them to 'serve' and why.
2. Consider members who are not in your industry.
3. Serve on someone else's personal board of advisors.

Exploration

Personal board prompts:
fill in the person(s) for each role on your personal board of advisors and what their motivation is to help you, including your cheerleader (supporter), coach (mentor), champion (advocate), connector (networker), and critic (truth teller). Then write a list of the people who you would like to see or affirm on your personal board of advisors.

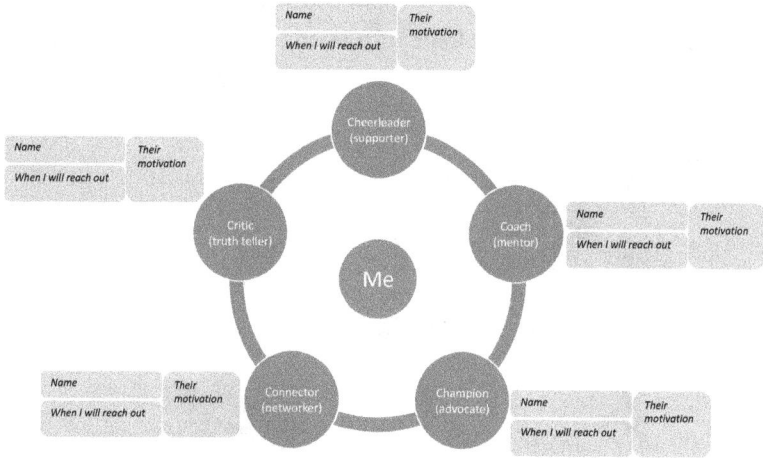

Figure 2.2 Personal board of advisors

#21 Conflict: Discord Style

Evidence

The word 'conflict' may raise your hackles, activating a neurobiological response that you would do almost anything to avoid. After all, your brain wants to keep you safe. Conflict is inevitable. How you respond to conflict is based on personality and social motives (Macintosh and Stevens 2008).[10] Finding five typical ways people tend to respond to conflict in the workplace, Kenneth Thomas and Ralph Kilmann created the Thomas Kilmann Conflict Model Instrument (TKI) on how people are willing to cooperate and how assertive to be with their goals.[11]

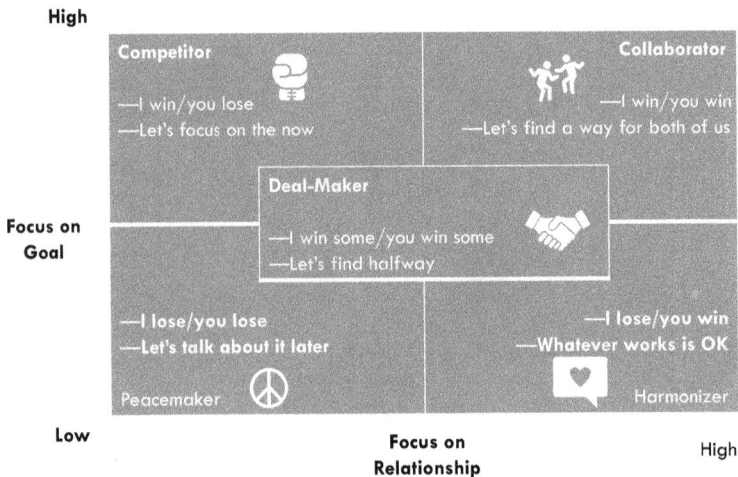

Figure 2.3 Conflict style

While you likely employ different styles and tactics depending on the context, you likely have a default style. Importantly, there is no "better" style than another. Knowing when and how to be flexible enables you to navigate different types of conflict. Awareness of your default style is an important place to start.

Experimentation

1. Pay attention to the context to flex your style.
2. Try out a style that is not your default.
3. Observe what another person's style may be.

Exploration

Conflict style questionnaire:
based on the Thomas–Kilmann Conflict Inventory, this questionnaire is an indicator, not a definitive assessment. Put your rating for each line on a scale of 1 to 4: 1 = rarely, 2 = sometimes, 3 = often, and 4 = always.

Statement	No.	Rating
I explore issues with others to find solutions that meet everyone's needs.	1	
I try to negotiate and adopt a give-and-take approach to problems.	2	
I try to meet others' expectations.	3	
I argue my case and insist on the merits of my point of view.	4	
I gather as much information as I can and keep lines of communication open.	5	
I usually say very little and try to leave a situation as soon as possible.	6	
I try to see disagreements from both sides and understand the issues.	7	
I prefer to compromise when solving problems and move on.	8	
I find conflicts challenging and exhilarating and enjoy a battle of wits.	9	
I get uncomfortable and anxious being at odds with other people.	10	
I try to accommodate the wishes of my friends and family.	11	
I can figure out what needs to be done, and I am usually right.	12	
I meet people halfway to break deadlocks.	13	
I may not get what I want, but it's a small price to pay for keeping the peace.	14	
I avoid hard feelings by keeping my disagreements with others to myself.	15	

Conflict style scoring:

Put the rating to the corresponding No. Then add each row for a total.

No.	Rating	No.	Rating	No.	Rating	Total	Style
1		5		7			Collaborating
4		9		12			Competing
6		10		15			Peacemaker
3		11		14			Harmonizer
2		8		13			Dealmaker

Conflict styles:

Based on your highest (or two highest) scores by "total," review which conflict style may be your default style.

Collaborator	Competitor	Peacemaker	Harmonizer	Dealmaker
Meet in middle	Win-lose	Delay	Lose-win	Win-win
Fairness	Winning	Risk-averse	Relationship	Create value
Maximize	Adversary	Indecision	Yield	Concession
Honest	Aggressive	Passive	Appease	Cooperative

#22 Transform: Making Friends With Conflict

Evidence

Conflict in a team can signal a healthy work environment given the right conditions. Shifting from managing conflict to transforming conflict invites the possibilities and benefits of differences. In fact, when a workplace encourages differing opinions, the entire team benefits from the wisdom of diverse perspectives.[12] Studies show groups that encourage healthy conflict engender trust, cohesiveness, and performance. To achieve this, teams must have a shared understanding that conflict is positive and resolvable.[13] While it often seems easier to get things done if everyone simply agrees, there is no shortage of evidence that groupthink can stymy innovation and performance. For a team to avoid blind spots and missed opportunities, making space for productive friction is critical.

According to Linda Hill, creative abrasion is conflict that encourages debate and discourse to surface the ideas that fuel innovation.[14] When you transform conflict, you leverage the inherent wisdom within the team. Leveraging your conflict styles and understanding your context can better prepare you to shift from avoiding conflict to embracing it. Focusing on your values and highest intention for the discussion helps you and your team to shift from a fight about personalities and identities to a dialogue about possibilities.

Experimentation

1. Identify one thing that can get in the way of your listening.
2. Name for each other what might stop your team from finding a way forward.
3. Commit to one way to mitigate potential obstacles.

Exploration

Conflict prompts:
reflect on a current conflict you are encountering.

Your highest intention/hope for the outcome
Your values that you bring to this situation
The other people's values they bring to this
Your shared values
Useful perspectives you bring to this situation
Useful perspectives they bring to this situation
What possibilities exist for healthy disagreement
What possibilities exist for shared understanding

Conflict style prompts:

Your default conflict style
How appropriate is this style for this situation
What happens if you overdo your style
What you know about the other person's style
The context that you should be aware of
What a helpful conflict style is in this situation

#23 Boundaries: Just Say No

Evidence

Like many people, you likely hate to say no. Even if it's something you don't want to do or know it's not good for you, you probably don't like to disappoint or hurt the other person's feelings. Perhaps you fear conflict, or that the person will see it as rejection of them, or that person will not help you down the line. Researchers have found that people tend to overindex the possibilities of a negative reaction because they want so badly to avoid any inkling of a less-than-positive response.[15] In many situations, they worry that saying no puts a hard stop on any future opportunities, that there is no second chance. Research supports what you likely know from experience: that boundaries are correlated with well-being.[16]

William Ury of the acclaimed *Getting to Yes* notes that boundary setting and saying no can be positive and powerful.[17] Whether navigating tough negotiations or making tough decisions, grounding yourself in your value system and knowing what is important to you is like having a deep root system of a tree that cannot be easily uprooted. Having this groundedness gives you clarity, strengthening your ability to say no when the choice conflicts with your values. You then have more fortitude to say no when it doesn't align with you. That allows you to set clear boundaries and say yes to the relationship or to future possibilities when you do find alignment.

Experimentation

1. Practice saying no to one thing.
2. Reflect on what the longer-term benefits of the relationship or opportunity are.
3. Do an inventory of what can be let go with a "no."

Exploration

Boundaries prompts:
reflect on a current dilemma or opportunity you are not sure how whether to say yes or no.

What you value	
How this dilemma/opportunity aligns with your values	What you will say yes to
How this dilemma/opportunity does not align with your values	What you will say no to
What possibilities exist (other opportunities, relationships) beyond this one dilemma or opportunity?	

#24 Groundedness: Eye of the Storm

Evidence

In the stormy chaos of change, it becomes that much more important for you to be like the eye of the storm, grounded in your values and clear on your North Star. Otherwise, you can easily get tossed by the storm or make the storm even more chaotic for those around you. Research has shown that leaders who are mindfully present without judgment have greater self-awareness and ability to regulate themselves and develop others. They are also less susceptible to being caught up by the pressures of changing winds and instead, be guided by a steadfast ethical compass on how to reach the North Star.[18]

When you are present, you are more centered and grounded, having more deliberate focus. From this place, you are more able to discern wiser decisions and role model what steady, authentic, and courageous leadership looks like. This then allows us to utilize and leverage our skills more effectively, especially during challenging times.[19]

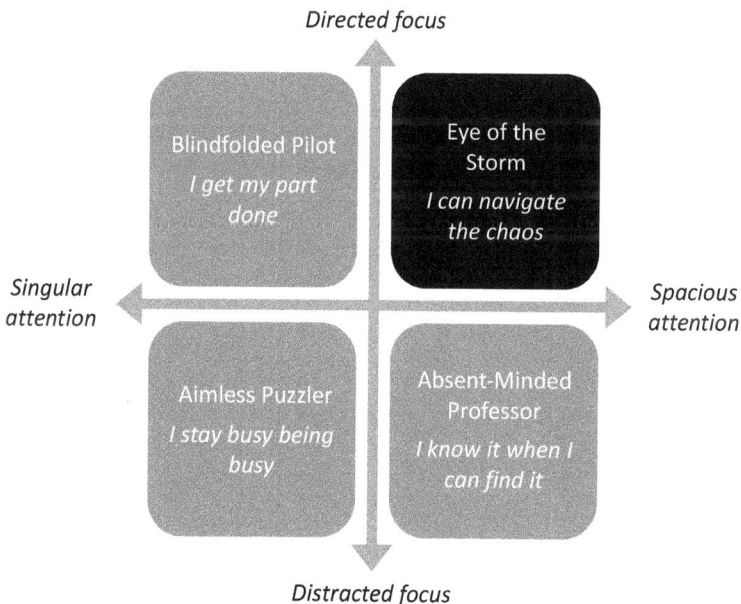

Figure 2.4 *Centeredness*

Experimentation

1. Practice a moment of mindfulness each day.
2. Observe the situation without having to act immediately.
3. Invite team members to share their values vis-à-vis this situation.

Exploration

Groundedness prompts:
reflect on a current change and situation of uncertainty.

What you are most worried or concerned about this…
What you are most excited or hopeful about this…
What values ground you/your team…
What your and your team's North Star is and how you stay on course…
The appropriate level of focus you need to bring—and when (how directed)…
The appropriate level of attention you need to bring—and when (how spacious)…

#25 Regulation: Fear and Change

Evidence

Your brain craves consistency. Consistency feels safe. When you are facing a change, even a positive one, your sense of safety is threatened, which can compromise your ability to respond wisely. This is because your autonomic nervous system (ANS) constantly scans your environment to detect potential dangers and kicks in to respond to fear. Its two main components regulate your physiological responses to keep you safe: (1) the sympathetic nervous system (SNS), known as the "fight or flight" response, and (2) the parasympathetic nervous system (PNS), known as the "rest and digest" response. The main (and largest) nerve of your PNS is the vagus nerve, which plays a central role in detecting and responding to stimuli. It acts like a brake on your SNS. According to Polyvagal Theory, there are three states of response to a potential threat:[20]

Dorsal vagal state	Shutdown	Immobilize to protect—dissociation
Sympathetic state	Fear	Mobilize to react—fight or flight
Ventral vagal state	Safety	Connect to engage—curiosity

Activating your vagus nerve through practices such as deep breathing, meditation, music, humming, and even laughing supports your ability to better regulate your ANS. The more you can regulate, the more you can make decisions on whether to accept or make, or how to best respond to a change from a place of safety rather than from a place of fear.

Experimentation

1. Pause before making or responding to a change and be aware of which state you are in.
2. Take longer exhales than inhales to stimulate your PNS.
3. Play music to activate your vagus nerve.

Exploration

Change prompts:
consider a change you are facing or a decision you need to make.

From what state you are examing this change (e.g., fear or safety)…

This change is scary because…
How real this fear is…
The worse thing that could happen with this change…
What you can do to mitigate or minimize potential 'cons…'

The positive aspects about this change….
The extent to how real these possibilities are…
What else you are curous about this change…
The best thing that could happen with this change….
Wat you can do to help mobilize these potential benefits…

Change decision prompts:

On a scale of 1–10, your level of regret if you don't make this change (1 = zero regret; 10 = major regret)
You are 95 years old. What you will tell yourself and your friends about the choice you made.

#26 Focus: Aperture Zoom

Evidence

Intentional and deliberate focus enables you to simultaneously hold a past-present-future view. This orientation requires you to hold both zooming in on the present while zooming out to learn from history and look beyond tomorrow. Vijay Govindarajan proposes a "three-box solution," which selectively preserves what worked in the past, optimizes the present, and innovates for the future.[21] That is not easy to do because focusing on the minutiae of the everyday is tempting and can help you to feel productive and busy, especially when there are other overwhelming things calling for your attention that require more complex thinking and time. Yet a myopic view may limit your capacity to take a broader perspective and see things from a 30,000-foot view. On the other hand, if you go too big picture, you might have your head in the clouds such that you forget how your decisions impact a lot more than you may know.

The more positional power you have, the more distant you become from the frontline. Rosabeth Moss Kanter notes that effective leaders choose when and how they zoom out and when and how they zoom into the details.[22] Sometimes you have to run up to the 'balcony' to get a birdsye view, and other times, to the 'orchestra pit' to get into the weeds. Knowing where to attend your focus requires honest reflection of where you are, what you need, and what you're missing. Being deliberate about your focus enables you to become more impactful in the moment and in the long run.

Experimentation

1. Find one opportunity to zoom in and out.
2. Check with other stakeholders to learn from the past.
3. Check with other stakeholders to imagine the future.

Exploration

Focus prompts:

consider your current situation or challenge.

What really is happening - observable information rather than your or others' interpretations of what is happening…
What you need to know to move forward in this situation/overcome this challenge…
What you need to know that you don't right now? What is missing…

Zoom in, zoom out prompts:

first go up to "the balcony." Imagine you are observing from a distance as a third party or alien who sees the bigger picture without judgment or attachment. Then go to the "orchestra pit." Imagine you are immersed in the experience.

	View from the balcony	**View from the orchestra pit**
Situation: facts		
Benefits: gains		
Opportunities: possibilities		
Obstacles: barriers		
Drawbacks: cons		
Must-haves: non-negotiables		
Absolute nos: dealbreakers		

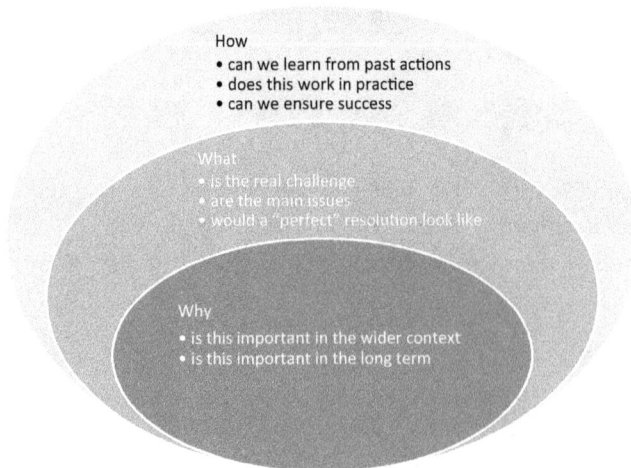

How
- can we learn from past actions
- does this work in practice
- can we ensure success

What
- is the real challenge
- are the main issues
- would a "perfect" resolution look like

Why
- is this important in the wider context
- is this important in the long term

Figure 2.5 Zoom in/out

Zoom action prompts:

reflecting on the questions above that apply to you, consider how you want to approach the situation, what the core issues are, what your goals are, and why this is important.

How…	
What…	
Why…	

What to keep from the past…	
What to leave in the past…	
What the current possibilities are…	
How the future can look like…	

#27 Transition: The Messy Ice Cube

Evidence

Everyone moves through transitions differently, and honoring those differences is critical. Kurt Lewin's model of change calls this transition period the "moving" part of his unfreezing-moving-freezing framework. Like a melted ice cube before being put back into the freezer, there is a dismantling of what has been and a pool of messiness before the water refreezes, perhaps into a different shape. Lewin's framework recognizes this uncertain, messy period of the "in-between" and is the foundation of other models of change.[23]

Rather than rush to the refreeze period, it is important to honor the messiness, including the discomfort of transitions. This includes an acknowledgment, a mourning, of what you are losing, even if it's a "good" loss. Transitions require you to leave what is at least familiar. Because you have a human need for consistency, when there is a gap between what you knew and what is now, you may experience cognitive dissonance.[24] To avoid dissonance, you may over-rationalize or seek to find blame. But if you mourn the loss, sit with the discomfort, and be curious about it, you may be better prepared for the new normal.

Experimentation

1. Sit with the discomfort; don't rush to problem-solve.
2. Be explicit about mourning the loss of what was.
3. Share with someone else your commitment to honor your transition time.

Exploration

Transition prompts:
reflect on a change you are currently going through.

The beforetime…	
What it looked like	What it felt like
What you valued about it	What you didn't value about it

The in-between…	
What it looks like	What it feels like
What resources do you have during this time	What support do you need during this time
What you are losing	What you are gaining

The new normal…	
What it looks like	What it feels like
What you value about it	What you don't value about it
What resources do you need to embrace this	What support do you need to embrace this

#28 Change: Riding the Roller Coaster

Evidence

Ninety percent of executives say their businesses have fundamentally changed since 2020, requiring innovative and agile thinking.[25] Yet being nimble with change is not about the speed but your willingness to embrace it. Rather than fighting to get off the roller coaster of life, embracing the experience enables you to navigate the heart-dropping moments and the elevated highs with greater balance. One of the most influential works on how humans deal with the process of dying,[26] the Kübler-Ross model explores the five stages of grief when one faces a prognosis of terminal illness. While this model has received some criticism for its oversimplification and selective data, her framework is often misunderstood as a linear stage progression of dealing with someone else's death.

While death is a rather poignant type of change, people go through similar stages and emotions during other kinds of change. Of course, you do not go through emotions in a linear fashion; sometimes you skip ahead, and sometimes you revert. You also do not go through them in delineated time frames. There is also no "better" or "worse" stage. When you become more attuned to how your emotional experiences are inherently tumultuous and impermanent, you can more easily adopt a helpful mindset and behaviors that ease the process and journey.

Experimentation

1. Observe which parts of the curve you find yourself spending more time on.
2. Map out where each team member is.
3. Have a discussion with your team on how to acknowledge and work with where you are.

Exploration

Your change curve prompts:
Reflect on a current or recent change.

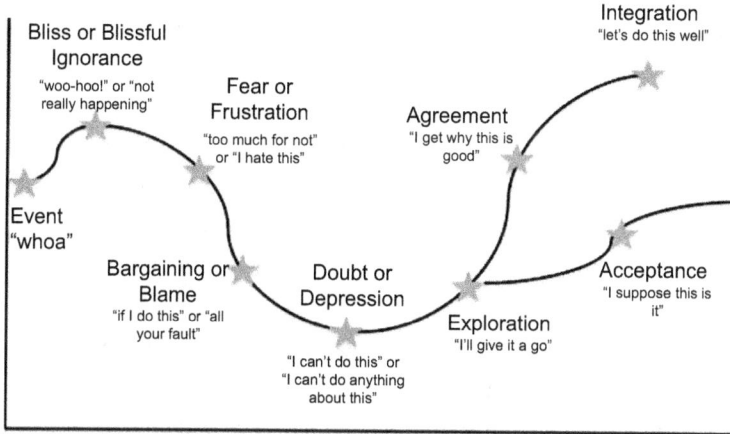

Kübler-Ross Emotional Change Curve

Figure 2.6 Change curve

Where you are on this curve and how you can tell
What factors influence your moving along or back along the curve
What factors keep you at a certain place
What you need to help you find greater acceptance or integration with the change

Team change curve prompts:
reflect on a current or recent change.

Where your team is on this curve and how you can tell
What factors influence your team's moving along or back along the curve
What factors keep your team at a certain place
What you can do to support your team to find greater acceptance or integration with the change

#29 Self-Efficacy: Adapting With Agency

Evidence

In the parable of the two arrows, the first arrow that hits you is out of your control. The second arrow, however, is self-inflicted and often comes in the form of self-judgment, self-criticism, or self-hatred. Negative self-talk can reduce your sense of self-efficacy, your belief that your actions have an impact on the outcome.[27] Especially during times of change, believing that you have agency, power, to make a difference, however small, is important to your resilience and ability to navigate uncertainty.

Having a sense of self-efficacy and agency cultivates the capacity for a more optimistic outlook where you can look for the possibilities and positives of experiences. Psychologist Martin Seligman doesn't equate such an optimistic outlook with being blissfully ignorant, but rather with the capacity to discern a sense of hope, gain important perspective, and have a sense of control.[28] Locus of control refers to how different people explain their sense of agency. Those who have an external locus of control tend to explain things as happening *to* them, avoiding any active part they could play. Research shows that those with an internal locus of control believe that they can affect what is happening and tend to have a stronger sense of agency, which is correlated with performance, well-being, and resilience.[29]

Experimentation

1. Pause before releasing the second arrow of self-judgment.
2. Reflect on your previous positive experiences where you felt you had agency.
3. Invite team members to reflect on their positive experiences where they had agency.

Exploration

Self-efficacy prompts:
reflect on a change you are currently facing.

On a scale of 1–5, rate how much of a threat (1) or opportunity (5) you see with this change	
What is realistically optimistic about this	
What is hopeful about this	
What is not within your control	
What is within your control	
What might get in the way	
What you will do to mitigate/minimize the block	
A helpful mindset (e.g., you adopt an attitude of generosity)	
A helpful behavioral response (e.g., you proactively volunteer to help)	
What action you will take	
Who/what will hold you accountable	

#30 Leading: Change CEO

Evidence

Seventy percent of organizational change initiatives fail.[30] Part of the difficulty is the number of variables that affect the likelihood of success, including a lack of perceived urgency, coalition stakeholder buy-in, vision, clear communication, alignment with culture, or attention to root issues. Leaders of companies that attune to mindset are four times more likely to lead successful transformation.[31] To understand mindsets, you must recognize where all your stakeholders may be in their willingness to support the change, including the quiet dissenters. You must pay attention to those who wait by the sidelines to see what happens, as they may have valuable insights on the barriers to adoption. It is also important not to assume your biggest cheerleaders for the change will always be your biggest cheerleaders. Being attentive to multiple perspectives is essential for success.

Leading organizational change requires a lot. However, it turns out it might not necessarily require convincing every person. A study of large-scale social change, for example, attitudes on gender equity, showed that 25 percent is the tipping point for it to be diffused across the system.[32] While social change is not the same as organizational change, leaders may focus on making the case to at least 25 percent of the population on why they will benefit financially, reputationally, and psychologically from adopting the behavioral change.

Experimentation

1. Pay attention to how much you are focusing on different stakeholders over others.
2. Check in with stakeholders to understand their mindsets throughout the transition.
3. Ask stakeholders to reflect on their vision, issues, sense of urgency, and barriers.

Exploration

Leading change prompts:
reflect on a change you are leading.

Vision: what the future look like…
Values: how this aligns with your organization's values
Stakeholders: how they perceive the vision; what they care about; what they are worried about
Issue: what the root cause/issue this change is addressing
Urgency: why this change is needed now
Action: what you need to make this happen
Barriers: what might get in the way
Communication: what and to whom you need to communicate this change

Stakeholder mindsets prompts:
consider who makes up your supporters (cheerleaders), your balanced or non-committals (neutrals), your vocal opposers (active dissenters), and your passive or stubborn refusers (quiet dissenters). Reflect on their perspectives, their concerns, and their benefits from this change.

Cheerleaders	
Neutrals	
Active dissenters	
Quiet dissenters	

#31 Impact: The Leader Touch

Evidence

Impact is not the same as intention. Undoubtedly, you have experienced moments where your intention had the opposite impact on someone else. Undoubtedly, you have been on the receiving end. This impact can be a result of words, actions, or even emotions. As with any contagion, emotions too have a contagious effect on a team. Emotional contagion is the tendency to mimic expressions, movements, and vocalizations to "converge emotionally" with another person.[33] People do not live or work as islands. They are affected, even unconsciously, by their team member's moods and emotions. At the group level, the impact can be profound, including performance, teamwork, conflict, and decision making.[34] Negative emotions beget negativity. Positive emotions beget positivity.

While emotional contagion happens bi-directionally between leader and follower and across teams, what leaders say and do have a broader ripple effect on their teams. They must pay attention to the energy they bring and to what they say and how they say it. A tonal inflection may heighten concerns. An inadvertent eyebrow raise may raise alarm bells. While you cannot overly script your words or facial expressions, being more explicit and transparent about your intentions may also minimize others' tendencies to make assumptions.

Experimentation

1. Practice what you want to say with a few different audiences.
2. Proactively ask your team how they receive what you say.
3. Ask others what their intention is, instead of jumping on assumptions.

Exploration

Influence and impact prompts:
reflect on a current message you need to deliver.

Your highest intention	
What you want to say	
What you need to say	
Who you need to say it to	
The impact you want to have	
What might their assumptions be about this	
Who else may hear it, and what impact you want to have	

What you will say	
How you will say it	
When you will say it	
What you will do to make your intention explicit and transparent	
What your body language will say about your intention	
What your emotional expresssions will say about your intention	
What you will do it/when you don't have the intended impact you want	

#32 Challenge: Raise the Issue

Evidence

Having tough conversations is never easy. Whether communicating a change or navigating conflict, your mindset going into these conversations has a tremendous impact on the result. Adopting a mindset of inquiry and a spirit of connection increases your chances of a mutually desirable outcome. One helpful mindset is based on nonviolent communication (NVC), a communication process built on compassion, honest articulation and clarification of what you mean and what you want, and active and generous listening to understand.[35] Research on NVC shows that such an approach opens the door to authenticity[36] as well as empathy, conflict resolution, and well-being.[37] When you are authentic in how you communicate empathy, transparency, and a hopeful vision for the future, you are more likely to gain trust, belief, and engagement.[38]

Empathy in communication does not mean suppressing honesty or avoiding tough issues. When you attune to what is important for all parties, rather than only yourself, and do so with integrity, you can share difficult messages with greater equanimity.[39]

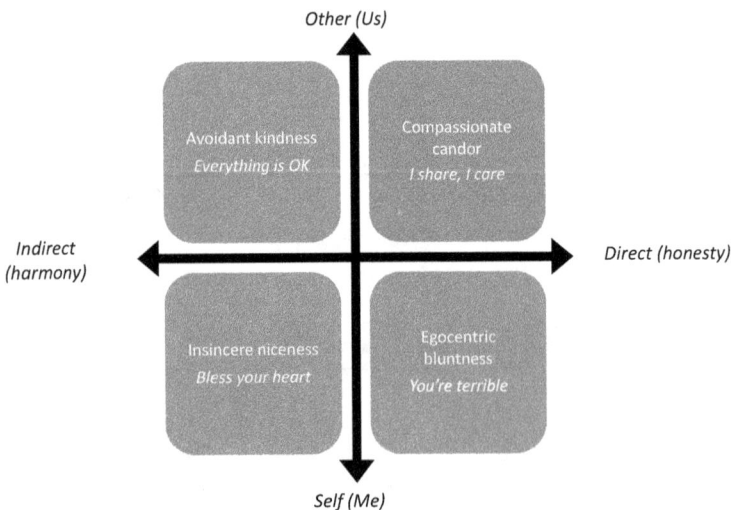

Figure 2.7 Compassionate candor

Experimentation

1. Practice being on the receiving end of tough messages and notice your response.
2. Create a norm and expectation for your team members to regularly raise concerns.
3. Proactively invite your team to first reflect on their intention and key message to deliver.

Exploration

Compassionate candor prompts:
reflect on a current tough situation or message you need to deliver.

Issue you want to raise or conversation you need to have

Facts of the situation …	
The impact of the issue on you, them, and others …	
How you feel about the situation …	
Your responsibility in the matter …	
What you hope to gain from the conversation …	
Three key points to address/main message in one sentence …	

The individual you need to speak with …	
Your relationship with this person …	
Potential obstacles to a productive conversation …	
How they may feel about the situation …	
What they may gain from the conversation …	

When and where you will hold the conversation …	
How you will start the conversation …	
How you will listen to the other person …	
How you will shift from judgment to curiosity …	
How you will manage their reactions …	
How you will stay present in the moment …	
How you will follow up …	

#33 Power: Managing Up

Evidence

In one study, 88 percent of participants said that managing up is important for their careers.[40] This isn't about just appeasing your boss, winning brownie points, or giving feedback. Managing up is about "creating value for your boss and your company."[41] It is about aligning your behavior and teams with that of the larger team in which you sit, which requires you to attune to our boss's needs, motivations, fears, pressures, and work styles.[42] Managing your boss can be tricky because power dynamics are at play, even in best-case scenarios.

The classic guidebook *Managing Your Boss* teaches that managing your boss builds a healthy relationship, mutual respect, and enables you to proactively learn, grow, and contribute.[43] To do so, knowing your and your boss's leadership style is helpful to better understand their motivations and behaviors. As most people are a combination of styles, Daniel Goleman's six types of leaders can be expanded to eight:

Judge	Makes decisions	Hands-free	Gives autonomy
Guardian	Follows rules	Connector	Prioritizes personal connection
Visionary	Inspires	Rocket	Sets the pace
Coach	Empowers others	Councilor	Diffuses decision making

Experimentation

1. Proactively ask your boss for what they see as their style, motivator, and needs.
2. Invite direct reports to share their perspectives about you.
3. Share your preferences with your direct reports.

Exploration

Power prompts:
reflect on your boss and others who hold more positional power or authority than you do, with whom you want to have stronger relationships.

	Supervisor	Leader 1	Leader 2
Position (role vis-à-vis me)			
Source of power/authority (title, budget, experience)			
Power style (default way to leading)			
Motivators (what drives them)			
Concerns (their pain points)			
Benefit (what you both gain)			
Need (what they need from you)			
Support (what you need from them)			
Value (what you bring that helps them)			
What you can control (what influence you have)			
What you cannot control (what is beyond your control)			
Tactic to better manage them (one commitment)			

#34 Feedback: Loop and Learn

Evidence

There is no shortage of research on the importance of feedback, yet it is one of the skills that most people find challenging—giving it and receiving it. Feedback is critical to your personal and professional development as it enables learning and mitigates conflict.[44] The challenge is doing it correctly. Overfocusing on negative feedback, being too prescriptive, focusing on "fixing," not involving the other person, or giving feedback too infrequently are all to be avoided.[45]

Some of the most important characteristics of good feedback include being grounded in strengths, focused on outcomes, and done frequently.[46] These include:

Situation	The context		Story	The emotions
Specific	The behavior		Synergy	The connection to the org
So what	The impact		Solution	The way forward

What you emphasize, when, and how you deliver it also depends on what kind of feedback it is: constructive, reinforcing, upward, formal, performance review, or in-the-moment.

Experimentation

1. Follow up after the feedback conversation.
2. Implement 1:1 formal feedback and regular, continuous feedback.
3. Proactively ask for feedback on yourself using the same template.

Exploration

Feedback Prompts:
reflect on feedback you want/need to share.

Who you are giving this to	
Type of feedback	
What you want them to think/feel/do	

Situation (what happened)	
Specific (what was the observable behavior)	
So what (the impact)	
Story (what you felt; what they/others felt)	
Synergy (how this relates to your organization and work)	
Solution (what commitment they make; how to move forward)	

When you will have this conversation	
Where you will have this conversation	
How you will start the conversation	
How you will know it is effective	
How you will follow up	

CHAPTER 3

Integration and Action

Encouraging Strategic Innovation

This module focuses on influencing and optimizing teams for transformation.

As teams go through transformation, whether large, organization-wide, or small, iterative ones, there must be an element of trust and psychological safety. You are better positioned to lead and navigate a successful transformation by optimizing and leveraging the strength and wisdom of the group. This requires a healthy organizational and team culture and climate, which is boosted by acknowledging and surfacing things that might get in the way, including assumptions and biases. It requires you to embrace existing and inherent tensions. Inviting divergent thinking and different perspectives encourages the discernment of the root causes and conditions of challenges presented and future-forward thinking. How you then communicate transformation through powerful language and stories will increase your capacity to influence and inspire innovation.

These 18 worksheets support you through the process of team culture and climate, perspective taking, and influence through a leadership point of view.

#35 Trust: Stronger Bonds

Evidence

According to David Maister and Charles Green, trust is derived from three components: credibility (you know what you're doing), consistency (you do what you say), and connection (you are approachable).[1] What takes away from trust is the presence of self-interest. Of course, everyone has their personal agendas, but a shared agenda is essential. Trust is the foundation of a healthy work environment and healthy relationships and relies on a sense of security with someone else. Security is generally based on a sense of someone's knowledge, character, action, or some combination of those aspects. Trusting someone does not necessarily overlap with friendship; airplane passengers trust a pilot because they have thousands of hours of training, not because they're friends.

What engenders trust with one person does not apply to everyone else. Trust is a two-way street; not only do you need to understand how much you trust them, but you also need to consider how much they trust you. As a leader, your positional power alone may impact what kind of trust is needed for different team members, who likely need something different from you to build trust. As such, you need to consider the extent to which they need attention and in what ways so that you can meet your mutual needs.

Experimentation

1. One action you can take to build someone else's trust in you.
2. One action you can take to build your trust in someone else.
3. Have a discussion on trust across your team.

Exploration

Trust prompts:

reflect on your team members, including those who you report to, your peers, and those who report to you. Rate the level (1 = low; 5 = high) of how much trust you have in each other and what they need from you to build trust.

	Person	Person	Person
Type of relationship (up, sideways, down)			

Level of trust you have in them (1 = low; 5 = high)			
Credibility			
Consistency			
Connection			
Self-motivation			

Level of trust you think they have in you (1 = low; 5 = high)			
Credibility			
Consistency			
Connection			
Self-motivation			

Level they need from you (1=low; 5 = high)			
Praise			
Protection			
Collaboration			
Involvement			
Personal connection			

Your commitment to build trust with them			

#36 Safety: Stages of Expression

Evidence

Your need to feel safe is biologically wired into your autonomic nervous system; you must feel safe before you can be open to anything else.[2] Psychological safety, which has been researched for more than 80 years, refers to a shared experience and understanding that makes it possible to voice concerns and take risks without fear of repercussions or judgment. Research consistently shows that a judgment-free environment, where people feel safe to voice concerns and take risks, creates the conditions for the most productive, engaged, and high-performing teams.[3]

Remember that those in positional power may report greater psychological safety than those who report to them.[4] Gender and race also come into play. How you experience psychological safety is likely different than others, even on the same team. Timothy Clark examines four stages that individuals may experience depending on context: feeling included, learning, contributing, and challenging.[5] Paying attention to these different dynamics will help you to attend to the areas where someone may feel less safe.

Experimentation

1. Observe patterns and trends by context and by person.
2. Notice behavioral indicators of where someone might be on the levels.
3. Have 1:1s to understand why each person is at which stage.

Exploration

Psychological safety prompts:
consider the people on your team and the context in which you and they may experience different types of psychological safety. This is based on Timothy Clark's four stages.[6] Reflect on the behavioral indicators that suggest the extent to which you and they may experience each form of psychological safety. Do this for a few different contexts.

Context 1			
	You	**Person 1**	**Person 2**
Stage 1: Inclusion *You feel like you belong*			
Stage 2: Learner *You are open to learning*			
Stage 3: Contributor *You want to contribute*			
Stage 4: Challenger *You speak up*			

Context 2			
	You	**Person 1**	**Person 2**
Stage 1: Inclusion *You feel like you belong*			
Stage 2: Learner *You are open to learning*			
Stage 3: Contributor *You want to contribute*			
Stage 4: Challenger *You speak up*			

#37 Accountability: Eyes on You

Evidence

The Workplace Accountability Study found that 80 percent of 40,000 survey participants believe accountability to be synonymous with negative feedback given only when something goes wrong. It found that most people (85 percent) say they weren't sure what their goals were, and even more (93 percent) say they don't know how to take accountability.[7] Furthermore, 82 percent of leaders don't feel empowered to hold others accountable.[8] After all, it is easy to set goals when no one knows about them. No one will know whether you did it or not. This is why accountability surfaces so much anxiety and resistance.

Yet accountability goes hand in hand with psychological safety. Psychological safety does not mean 'anything goes.' Environments where people do anything they want can turn into an overly permissive place where toxicity can fester. Rather, psychological safety with accountability creates what Amy Edmundson calls the "learning zone."[9] To learn and grow, you must feel safe to take risks and make mistakes *and* be responsible for your words and actions. Instead of viewing accountability as only a negative, when you reframe accountability as a gift, it can have a positive impact on performance, productivity, and engagement. It is a sign that you honor the other person's time and contributions, give recognition when they meet or exceed expectations, and offer clarity when they don't.

Experimentation

1. Find an accountability partner.
2. Commit to offering positive check-ins to let others know what is and isn't working.
3. Have a conversation with the team on what they can do to hold each other accountable.

Exploration

Accountability prompts:
consider the people on your team and the level of clarity they have on the following to create greater accountability.

	Person 1	Person 2	Person 3
Understanding and alignment of mission, vision, and values			
Standards of behavior			
Clarity of role			
Clarity of goals and outcomes			
Shared buy-in: how to achieve goals and outcomes			
Understanding of consequences of not meeting expectations			
Milestones			
How and when you check in (how and when)			
How to address mistakes			
How to encourage learning			
How you give feedback			
How they give feedback			
How to honor accomplishments			

#38 Contract: The Unwritten Rules

Evidence

You go into employment contracts making sure that all the 'i' s are dotted and 't's are crossed. What you might miss, however, is the psychological contract. This is not generally written or stated anywhere, but it is an important part of how one feels about the arrangement. Does the arrangement feel fair? Equitable? Supportive? Born out of the concepts of reciprocity and social exchange, the notion of a psychological contract emerged as to how to understand the terms of the reciprocal relationship with their employer.[10]

The challenge with a psychological contract is explicitly aligning the expectations of the employer and employee. It is important to spell out a range of issues that might otherwise be assumed, from career development to job security to work–life balance. Without making these terms explicit, things will go swimmingly well … until they don't. For example, someone on your team has long assumed that working three years garnered a promotion, while you assumed they were aware that certain milestones had to be reached, irrespective of tenure. While years one and two may have transpired without much incident, not being promoted in year three may leave one or both parties feeling like the other directly broke what they believe was a promise. The more you make these expectations explicit, the better you are at preempting potential fissures.

Experimentation

1. Consider how each contract looks differently with different people and relationships.
2. Make the contract explicit and easy to access.
3. Review the contract every six months.

Exploration

Supervisor psychological contract prompts:
consider the areas you want to raise with your supervisor to make a more
explicit psychological contract.

Organization (how your supervisor sees the current business situation and your role within it)	
Expectations (from you and your team members as it relates to goals, job performance)	
Goals (short-, medium-, and long-term goals—yours, theirs, and your team's)	
Resources (what support you need and where to find it)	
Working style (how you work, how they work, and what you need to support each other)	

Team psychological contract prompts:
consider the areas you want to raise with your team to make a more explicit
psychological contract. Give this to your team members so they can cocreate
one with you.

Organization (how you see the current business situation and their role within it and how they see it)	
Expectations (from you as it relates to goals, job performance)	
Goals (short-, medium-, and long-term goals—yours, theirs, and your team's)	
Resources (what support they need and where to find it)	
Working style (how they work, how you work, and what you need to support each other)	

#39 Culture: Climate Check

Evidence

A global study found that 72 percent of over 3K leaders say that culture helps successful transformation to happen, and 66 percent of executives say that culture is more important than strategy (PricewaterhouseCoopers, 2021).[11] PricewaterhouseCoopers identifies "culture enablers" that support organizations to use their culture as a competitive advantage, including the messaging from senior leadership, the use of technology, incentives and benefits, development and training, and employee networks.[12] However, paying attention to culture alone is insufficient. Whereas organization or team cultures are the norms and behaviors that shape how individuals interact and make decisions, organizational or team climate addresses the current experience of individuals. Climate refers to how they feel about and perceive the workplace and is influenced by several things, including leadership styles, communication, and work pressure. The former is the longer-term, invisible code; the latter is a shorter-term pulse check.

Paying attention to both culture and climate enables you to be aware of the immediate, more mutable perceptions of team members, which impact the norms. When they are not, retention and disengagement are at risk. For example, the team culture emphasizes well-being, but team members experience being expected to respond to emails 24/7. On the other hand, when culture and climate are aligned, engagement and performance are boosted.

Experimentation

1. Take a temperature "pulse check" at the start of each meeting.
2. Take a regular "pulse check" survey of current attitudes and experiences.
3. Review the contract every six months.

Exploration

Culture prompts:
consider your team member's expectations of the following areas.

Your team's core values and team member's expectations for living out these values? What are your team member's expectations for living out these values?	
Your team member's expectations for psychological safety and accountability?	
Your team member's epectations for transparency and communication?	
What are your team member's expectations for training and development?	
What are your team member's expectations for well-being?	
What are your team member's expectations for diversity and inclusion?	

Climate prompts:
consider how your team members are experiencing these areas in the moment.

How your team members are living out your team's core values?	
How your temembers are experiencing psychological safety and accountability?	
How your temembers are experiencing transparency and communication?	
How your temembers are experiencing training and development?	
How your temembers are experiencing well-being?	
How your temembers are experiencing diversity and inclusion?	

Culture and climate prompts:

Where there is misalignment between your team's culture and climate…	
Where there is alignment…	
What you will do to find greater alignment …	

#40 Charter: Becoming a Team

Evidence

Teams may start out with a clear "North Star," but time pressures and competing priorities can easily lead team members astray. While there are different ways of mapping out team roles and responsibilities, such as a RACI or GANTT chart, a team charter can help teams stay clear and committed to how they want to work together. This allows teams to stay focused on their "North Star" and how to hold each other with trust and accountability. Research suggests that a map of roles and responsibilities is useful to communicate values and expectations, build cooperation, and support them to manage conflicts.[13] The key is to ensure that all team members are involved in its creation and evolution.

When you are part of or leading a team, the likelihood is that the constellation of team members changes, or the set of tasks or deliverables shifts. It therefore becomes even more critical that you make these roles and responsibilities explicit because it is often the small details and misinterpretations that can lead a team member astray. It might feel like there is no time or need to revisit what seems like basic things, such as a document's version control. Yet these seemingly "small" things can become far bigger issues that will inevitably get in the way of optimizing the team's strengths. Taking time to continue iterating and making things explicit can avoid small misunderstandings from having a disproportionate impact.

Experimentation

1. Dedicate time to cocreate a team charter.
2. Make the team charter visible to everyone.
3. Continuously examine and update the team charter.

Exploration

Team charter prompts:

Your team's North Star…	
Your team's mission…	Your team's values…

Characters: what roles each of you play	
Communication: how often you meet, and how you communicate	
Content: who manages the knowledge and information	
Choices: how you make decisions, and who makes the decisions	
Concerns: how you surface and address concerns	
Conflict: how you raise conflict	

#41 Collective: Wisdom of the Group

Evidence

With teams, there is a synergy that transcends any individual. Collective intelligence (CI) refers to a group of people working together as one unit,[14] where there is coordination amongst the members such that the group's wisdom outpaces that of any one individual.[15] Interestingly, a team's CI is not the average of individual intelligence but is correlated with the social sensitivity of the group, how much each person has an opportunity to talk, and the presence of women.[16] The more team members are attuned to each other, the more CI and ability they must solve complex problems.

Of course, with any group, biases occur. Examples include groupthink (all congregate toward one opinion), anchor (what was said first becomes the baseline), and social loafing (defer to the others to act).[17] It is important for you to first be aware of your own potential biases and what role you play to boost and block the team. Being open to our thought process and emotional experiences can build transparency and trust. It is also important for you to be vigilant about the consistency of your team members' actions and when biases may creep in and compromise how well they work with each other. Checking into their thought processes and emotional experiences can also encourage the willingness to share what they know and what they do not know, opening the space for the group to collectively learn.

Experimentation

1. Acknowledge and encourage healthy team behaviors.
2. Offer different ways to solicit input from team members.
3. Role model giving and receiving feedback.

Exploration

Team relationship prompts:

How strong the relationships are within your team	How much trust you have within your team
How attuned you are to your own emotional states	How attuned your team is to each other's own emotional states
How attuned your team is to your needs	How attuned you are to each other's own needs
How attuned you are to your weaker areas	How attuned your team is to each other's weaker areas

Team communication prompts:

How effective your team is to think through problems together	How effective your team is to make decisions together
How effective your team is to surface tensions	How effective your team is to give each other feedback
How comfortable your team is to embrace conflict	How comfortable your team members are to embrace conflict

Team change readiness prompts:

How effective your team is to execute	How effective your team is to drive transformation
How aware you are of your responses to change	How aware your team is of each other's response to change
How invested you are to the change/project	How invested your team members are to the change project

#42 Team: Bench Strength

Evidence

Studies show that when there is a convergence between individual strengths and those of their team roles and their teams, there is a positive correlation with satisfaction and performance.[18] According to the VIA Institute on Character, team roles generally fall into one of seven: idea creator, informational gatherer, decision maker, implementer, influencer, energizer, and relationship manager.[19] While you likely play more than one of these roles at different times, you also probably have a natural strength in one or two. Knowing what yours are and that of your teams can help you to draw even more strength from the collective.

With over three-quarters of individuals in the United States alone working in matrixed teams, where they report to multiple leaders, Gallup has found that strengths-based teams adopt a mindset that holds everyone accountable and take the time to understand the team's collective strengths to develop and leverage their talents. This builds trust and clarity on how to better allocate tasks that best optimize strengths and talents.[20] Building on a team's collective strength also acknowledges and leverages the inherent diversity among individuals.[21] Understanding what strengths individuals on a team bring and how these strengths engage with each other can amplify and maximize the impact of that strength.

Experimentation

1. Observe behaviors to better identify your team's strengths.
2. Reflect how team successes reflect your team's strengths.
3. Find one opportunity each week to leverage your team's strengths.

Exploration

Team strengths prompts:
identify the key strengths of each team member and when their strengths may best serve them in different roles.

	Team member 1	Team member 2	Team member 3
Strengths			
Idea creator			
Informational gatherer			
Decision maker			
Implementer			
Influencer			
Energizer			
Relationship manager			

Strengths of your team as a whole…
Strengths your team is overdoing…
Strengths your team is underutilizing and could leverage more to achieve your team purpose…

	What is important to your team	What your team currently has	What your team needs
Talents—what your team is naturally good at			
Skills—capabilities your team can develop			
Knowledge—expertise your team has			

What makes your team uniquely strong…
What your team brings that is needed in your organization…
How you can help sustain and optimize your team's collective strengths…

#43 Bias: Under the Surface

Evidence

Mental shortcuts, or heuristics, speed up information intake, a survival instinct that is primarily unconscious. This means, you don't always know what you don't know.[22] Like most humans, you make assumptions from time to time. Your brain likes to put things (and people) into categories to make sense of information overload and to inform how you might behave. The trick is remembering that such assumptions are arbitrary. For example, in one study, a photo of a person shown along with a famous athlete makes viewers assume that the person is also athletic, even without evidence.[23] People craft stories about people, based on many different contexts, but if you're not careful, these stories can be harmful.

Although it is not usually intentional, unexplored mental heuristics and shortcuts can lead to unconscious bias that can be self-limiting or harmful to others. Biases are neither good nor bad. However, it is irresponsible to trick yourself into believing that your decisions are purely "rational, data-driven" or to exempt yourself from the need to be more aware of how bias creeps into everything, from recruitment to project allocation. It is therefore critical to actively work and help yourself and your teams get curious about and surface the hundreds of cognitive biases that may creep in and negatively impact how you work with each other.[24]

Experimentation

1. Proactively observe and mitigate a bias each week.
2. Ask for others to give feedback or call you out on bias.
3. Commit to calling out biases for each other.

Exploration

Bias prompts:

consider the biases that tend to or may creep into:

How your team hires	
How your team makes decisions	
How your team does performance reviews	
How your team chooses project teams	
How your team mentors others	
How your team supervises others	
How your team collaborates	
How your team gives feedback	
How your team chooses project teams	
How your team assigns work	
How your team learns and develops	
How your team gives recognition	

#44 Reframe: Team Triggers

Evidence

A trigger usually refers to a sensory reminder of a traumatic event. Even though there may be no imminent danger, your brain makes an unconscious association of that previous experience with stimuli—certain words, smells, sounds, and the like. Your brain then stores that away, and when you are confronted with that stimulus, it can trigger a strong emotional response. If you're not mindful, the response is grounded in feeling threatened and can lead you to the fight–flight–freeze–fawn response. In the workplace, you can be triggered by reminders of previous professional experiences, such as a public humiliation by our boss or a colleague disagreeing with you on a value that you hold dearly.

In teams, the likelihood of triggers becomes a multiple of multiples, leading to teamwide confusion. How one person responds to an email may inadvertently activate a bad memory from another, leading to unfounded distrust or dislike. Being able to notice and manage your and your team's triggers is critical to preempt potential problems. By pausing and reframing a different way to relate to that memory, you have a better chance to regulate your and your team's emotional responses, which will hopefully lead to healthier team dynamics.[25]

Experimentation

1. Proactively ask for each person to share what triggers them.
2. Commit as a team to openly speak about triggers.
3. Commit as a team to discuss more useful responses together.

Exploration

Your trigger prompts:

reflect on possible triggers that might activate you and your team, your natural reaction is, assumptions you are making about that trigger, how you can reframe the trigger to something more useful, and what a healthier response may be.

Trigger	Reaction (think/feel/do)	Assumptions	Reframe	Useful response (think/feel/do)

Team trigger prompts:

identify potential moments that might trigger your team and lead to conflicts (e.g., interruptions), how the team might likely react, and how you might help them to reframe such trigger.

Moment	Reaction (think/feel/do)	Reframe	Support

#45 Vision: Come With You

Evidence

Most people seek leaders who are forward-looking.[26] Having a vision and connecting team member's work with the bigger picture increases employee satisfaction,[27] which is positively correlated with commitment, productivity, and profitability. When you find alignment with what you care about, you are more likely to put in the effort. As a leader, you may create the vision, and you are also responsible for communicating it in such a way that others around it can believe it and feel empowered by it.

Noel Tichy describes great leaders as great teachers. His leadership point of view (LPOV) framework encourages leaders to examine three components to help create a shared vision that inspires and gets buy-in from others: (1) idea—shared vision of why you do what you do, (2) values—shared understanding of how you bring the idea to life, and (3) emotional energy/edge—shared momentum of what excites you and others and the courage to make tough and wise decisions.[28] When you are clear in your leadership point of view, others are clearer of what you're trying to achieve, where you want to take them, and why they should follow you.

Experimentation

1. Simplify your vision in a simple, compelling message.
2. Practice your leadership point of view with different audiences.
3. Identify who can be the best advocates and messengers of your vision.

Exploration

Leadership point of view prompts:

> IDEA: you/your team's shared vision; your WHY; what the future looks like

> VALUES: how you/your team brings your values to life; your shared understanding; how this aligns/reflects your values

> EMOTIONAL ENERGY: what motivates others; what creates a sense of urgency; why this is worthy of your/your team's time
> EDGE: what needs to be decided; what concrete actions you/your team needs to take

> In one sentence, your leadership point of view:

#46 Narrative: The WOW Factor

Evidence

If a leader's job is to influence, then few techniques are more effective than building a compelling narrative. A clear narrative helps to build your credibility[29] and capacity for optimal influence and inspiration, turning your vision into knowledge that motivates others to act. It is a consistent message that gives others information about "who you are ... where you've been, where you are, and where you are going."[30]

Crafting and articulating your narrative isn't as simple in practice, however. Your narrative is the big arc that gets individuals to understand the current reality and what Nancy Duarte calls "the new bliss," the wondrous future they will experience if they come along with you.[31] Your narrative is the common thread, woven together with stories and metaphors tailored to inspire different audiences and moments to overcome the inevitable barriers and obstacles that stand in the way of the current reality and the new bliss.[32] Knowing your audience will help you to understand what stories would be most meaningful for them and bring them behind a shared purpose and vision on a journey they are inspired to say, "Wow! Yes, I'm coming with you!"

Experimentation

1. Consider a few stories that fit your narrative that could be tailored to different audiences.
2. Ask different stakeholders whether they resonate with your narrative.
3. Ask different stakeholders how their stories fit into your narrative.

Exploration

Vision narrative prompts:

The vision you want to communicate...	
What this vision say about you/your team...	
The current reality: the problems, how big is this problem, and how does this vision address the problem...	
What the future looks like...	
What obstacles/challenges may arise as you move toward this future...	
The narrative of this vision to motivate others to act? (e.g., this team has the willpower and the waypower to make the cost of a lifesaving drug less than a cup of coffee if you cast aside our myopic tactics, remove short-term distractions, and bring a laser-sharp focus)	

Narrative audience prompts:

Who you want to influence...	
What do you know about them...	
Their current reality? How they experience the current problems...	
What the future look like for them if they come along this journey with you...	
What obstacles/challenges may arise for them as they move toward this future...	
What stories and examples would be meaningful for them that fit with your narrative...	

#47 Perspective: POV Taking

Evidence

Since 2020, 90 percent of executives say their businesses have fundamentally changed, requiring innovative and agile thinking.[33] This kind of thinking requires you to step into the shoes of your stakeholders to understand their viewpoints. Research shows that your ability to do so leads to stronger collaboration, creativity, and conflict management.[34] Doing so can shake you out of your default ways of thinking, especially when working in the same teams or with the same clients. Because brains like to categorize and grasp onto the first thing they hear (anchoring effect and priming effect), you and your team likely tend to converge your collective thinking without interrogation. Brains want the predictive nature of A + B = C.

Yet it is the unpredictability that fosters innovation. Research shows that diversity in thinking begets creativity.[35] Edward de Bono's classic *Lateral Thinking* shows that diversity and unpredictability in thinking often give teams better ideas and get them to overcome their inherent biases.[36] By seeing challenges from different perspectives, such as from different levels of an organization from different industries, you not only get more diversity in thought, but also challenge your own "boxes," training your brain to be more flexible, curious, and connected.

Experimentation

1. Adopt a perspective that is outside of yours each day.
2. Invite everyone to take a perspective that is outside their default.
3. Proactively invite those outside your usual bubble for their insights.

Exploration

Perspective-taking prompts:
inspired by Edward de Bono's (2020) Six Thinking Hats, consider a current
challenge that your team is working on. Invite each person to take on one of
these perspectives and discuss the issue from that perspective. If you want, after
some time, rotate the perspectives so each person must look at the issue from
another perspective.

The current challenge:	
Detective: facts/information What your team knows. What data your team has…	Skeptic: Devil's advocate What might go wrong? Why this wouldn't work…
Optimist: benefits What strengths help your team and what the benefits are…	Emoter: intuition/feeling How the team feels. What your gut says…
Innovator: new ideas What else your team could do. Other ideas…	Planner: process What needs to happen? How your team is doing it…

#48 Paradox: Power in Tension Play

Evidence

In the Japanese martial art of archery, kyūdō, the position of "kai" is where the archer is in a full draw position. The key is a balance between tension and relaxation. The moment you tense up is the moment you lose power. Leaders must be able to embrace multiple truths and competing priorities without tensing up getting frozen in tension. In fact, research shows that a paradox mindset, "the extent to which individuals embrace and are energized by tensions," is correlated with innovation, thriving, tolerance for mistakes, out-of-box thinking, and comfort with conflicting opinions and information.[37] Leaders who say "yes, and" rather than "either, or" are more able to address reality and put the time and resources to navigate the tough stuff, rather than going for easy, band-aid solutions.

PricewaterhouseCoopers explored six contradictions leaders must embrace in an ever-turbulent environment: humility–confidence, strategy–execution, tradition–innovation, technology–human, global–local, and political–integrity.[38] They urged leaders to embrace these tensions to discern the wiser course of action to help steer their organizations through current and future crises that impact the entire ecosystem.

Experimentation

1. Identify one tension to intentionally embrace each week.
2. Highlight one tension to discuss with your team.
3. Map out tensions by area or challenge.

Exploration

Tension promps:

the empty column in the middle represents a spectrum.

draw an X on where on the spectrum you fall. For example, if you lean towards Long term horizon, your X will be more towards the right side. If you are half-way, your X will be right in the middle.

Humility: don't know all the answers		Confidence: can lead through
Strategy: think and plan		Execute: do
Tradition: focus on what you do well		Innovation: focus on the future
Technology: focus on tech (e.g., AI)		Human: center humanity
Global: impact beyond the immediate		Local: care for community
Political: address stakeholder needs		Integrity: stay steadfast to values

Organizational tension prompts:

reflect on the tensions that currently exist for your organization—fill in additional tensions not listed. The empty column in the middle represents a spectrum.

Draw an X on where on the spectrum you fall. For example, if you lean towards Long term horizon, your X will be more towards the right side. If you are half-way, your X will be right in the middle.

Short time horizon		Long time horizon
Oversight		Autonomy
Speed		Input from multiple sources
Employee performance		Employee well-being
Hierarchy		Collaboration
Profit		Sustainability

#49 Complexity: Root Causes

Evidence

Well before the global pandemic of 2020 accelerated the urgency for leaders to be agile,[39] Ronald Heifetz and Marty Linsky knew that organizations needed to be nimbler with their actions and decisions over two decades ago.[40] Casting aside the old top-down management mentality, they posed that an adaptive leadership approach enabled leaders to embrace change, experimentation, and innovation. Adaptive leaders are willing to get to the core issues and grapple with their complexities.

Heifetz and Linsky urged leaders to explore whether their challenges are technical or adaptive in nature. Technical challenges are those that are solvable. They are not necessarily easy to solve, but organizations have the processes and know-how to address them. Adaptive challenges are less clear and not easily solvable. They often connect to deeper systemic issues that require a shift in mindset, values, or belief. There is no previous policy or process to copy. They require leaders to step back, dig deep to find the root cause, and expose the inherent tensions. For example, putting together a performance review plan is typically a technical problem. There are templates and previous know-how. However, getting people who never had a consistent performance review plan to adopt and sustain one will likely surface issues and is an adaptive problem. Addressing these root issues, however, may pre-empt recurring issues.

Experimentation

1. Identify whether your other challenges are technical or adaptive.
2. Cultivate your emotional and social intelligence.
3. Proactively seek out opinions across and beyond your immediate circles.

Exploration

Challenge prompts:
consider a current challenge you are facing/leading.

It is technical / adaptative (pick one)…
The conditions that suggest to you that is the case?

Technical challenge prompts:
if your challenge is technical:

What worked before	
What did not worked before	
What existing policies/processes	
What resources you need to do this	
Where in the organization this is best addressed	
Who needs to be consulted and involved	

Adaptive challenge prompts:
if your challenge is technical:

The tensions	
Your or your team's beliefs about this are	
What you/your team needs to believe to address this	
Who needs to be consulted and involved	
Radical changes this requires	
What you/your team would need to give up	
What you/your team would need to adopt	
What you/your team can try	

#50 Influence: Change Communication

Evidence

Everyone is motivated by WIIFM: *what's in it for me?* Research shows that when it comes to work, work motivation is an interplay of your internal psyche and the external environment. Rooted in the Self-Determination Theory, everyone is motivated by both their inner worlds of accomplishment and satisfaction and the contextual aspects of financial reward and recognition.[41] For you to communicate change effectively, you also need to take the perspective of others to answer the WIFT question: what's in it for them?

Social perspective taking refers to how you perceive other's thoughts, feelings, and motivations.[42] While you will never truly know, you may be able to more accurately surmise by raising more emotional and social awareness and cultivating empathy to understand the other person's perspective. It turns out that the more positional power you have, the harder it becomes to have empathy for the other and the less accurately you become attuned to their viewpoints.[43] This means you must pay particular attention to understand, so that you can effectively tailor our communication to the other person's needs.

Experimentation

1. Invite a stakeholder to validate/clarify your questions.
2. Consider other stakeholders not on the list.
3. Tailor a communication strategy to each stakeholder.

Exploration

Change communication prompts:

The change/vision	Three words to describe the change/vision

Stakeholder influence prompts:
consider your range of stakeholders and consider the following from their perspective:

	Sponsors	Senior leadership	Supervisors/ managers	Peers	Direct reports/ frontline
Who					
Why they care					
Their concerns					
Their hopes					
What they gain					
What they lose					
What changes for them					
What they want to know					
What will help them to embrace it					

#51 Advocacy: Change Agents

Evidence

Change generally doesn't happen only to you. Even if you may have bought into and are ready for the change, you still need to communicate the change and identify the team members who are able and willing to amplify that communication further, getting buy-in and investment in the change.[44] These are the individuals who are best positioned to be your strongest advocates to convince others that they too will benefit from the change. As a leader, you must pay attention to various factors, including who on your team demonstrates the most proactivity and learning agility.[45] This means attending to how much your team members feel capable and resourced to adapt to changing situations, willing to take initiative and learn new competencies, and have the freedom to adjust their daily tasks to meet the new demands.

It is also helpful to first identify whether the organizational change is comprised of smaller, gradual changes, known as adaptive changes, such as new policy, or is a dramatic departure from the current modus operandi, known as transformative changes, such as an entirely new department.[46] Taking time to understand the emotional experiences of each team member will enable you to better address their concerns and leverage their excitement,[47] and identify those who are poised to be your biggest advocates.

Experimentation

1. Meet with each team member to uncover their perspectives and emotional experiences.
2. Ensure that the communication plan is aligned with your team's needs and concerns.
3. Attend to what needs to be adjusted to refine your messaging.

Exploration

Team change readiness prompts:
reflect on a current change you and your team are facing:

The extent to which the team is proactive...	The extent of flexibility your team has with their current roles
The extent to which the team knows about the change...	The extent to which the team is supportive about the change
The extent to which the team is equipped with the tools and skills to implement the change...	The extent to which the team is resistant to the change...
Who is responsible for providing the support this team needs...	The extent to which the team can sustain the change...

Change advocate prompts:
reflect on who may be best suited to support you as a change advocate:

Who is best positioned to get the word out about the change...	What this advocate needs to communicate effectively about the change...
The extent to which this advocate is proactive...	The extent of flexibility this advocate has with their current roles...
The extent to which this advocate knows about the change...	The extent to which this advocate is supportive about the change...
The extent to which this advocate is equipped with the tools and skills to implement the change...	The extent to which this advocate is resistant about the change...
Who is responsible for providing the support this advocate needs...	The extent to which this advocate can sustain the change...

#52 Audience: Brain on Stories

Evidence

Done well, communicating through stories captures hearts (affective) and minds (cognitive), drives greater trust and engagement, and inspires action.[48] From a neurobiological perspective, your brain responds to stories that are beyond your conscious understanding.[49] When you hear stories, cortisol is released to get your attention, oxytocin to build connection and empathy,[50] and dopamine for the reward. Stories stimulate your brain: right supramarginal gyrus (action-taking), left interior frontal gyrus (linguistic processing), interior frontal junction (visual processing), thalamus (intuition), Broca's area (speech), and Wernicke's area (auditory).

For stories to be effective, you must know your audience, what they care about, and what you want them to think/feel/do because of your story. The context helps you to choose the most appropriate structure, of which there are many, including origin (who you are), lessons (learning from mistakes), successes (demonstrating ability), connection (emotional resonance), real life (impact on customer), and imagine this (vision setting).

Experimentation

1. Practice your story out loud.
2. Tailor your story to different audiences.
3. Try a different story structure.

Exploration

Story prompts:

The message you want to communicate:	
WHY:	
This is important to you	This is important to the audience
WHO:	
You are and why you're the one to tell the story	The audience is to hear this story
HOW:	
This brings your values/ideas to life	This aligns with their values and interests
WHAT	
You want them to think/feel/do about you	You want them to think/feel/do about this

Structure of story
Story draft

Retrospection

As with most things, one size does not fit all. What is important is continued and consistent reflection, active inquiry, and commitment to action. This requires your belief that this is worth your investment of time and energy.

Most seasoned leaders will tell you they wished they paused more in their earlier career. Taking a pause does not equate to slowing down. In martial arts, it is the breath before a decisive strike. It builds your discipline and fortitude to set boundaries in a world of chaos and demands.

You know that it takes more than reading things once to be an effective future-forward leader of resilient teams. Keep this playbook somewhere where you can revisit when you need to, like calling on an old friend, only this is yourself as an effective coach. Stay on the journey:

- *Ground yourself.* It is your foundation for how you show up in the world.
- *Pause.* Reflect. Practice. Pause. Reflect. Practice. Rinse and repeat. Leading and working with intentionality and wisdom is a lifelong journey.
- *Keep this workbook as your companion.* Work on it by yourself, with a coach or client, with your teams, or all the above.
- *Tell someone.* Share your work with at least one person. Be accountable for taking action.
- *Get outside.* Being in nature is proven to benefit your brain and body. Walk through the woods; sit by a tree; watch a bird sing. Movement in nature soothes and stimulates.
- *Retrospect.* After you've tried some things out, take time to "look again." What went well? What made a positive difference? What didn't resonate? What unexpected factors came into place? What else do you want to know? What else do you want to ask?

As you operationalize and sustain your skills, let's look at three skills that can elevate the experience for yourself and others: powerful questions, active listening, and improvement.

Powerful Questions

You are likely a great problem solver. You ask the right questions to figure out the right action. You may also be less likely to wait for others to uncover their own solutions. Whether for yourself or others in working through a challenge or goal, consider a few types of questions:

Envision	What would success look like—what would you be saying and doing
Explore	What would you like to see that is different—what do you mean by…
Examine	What is your current belief—what might get in the way
Empower	What strengths do you bring—how might you reframe
Enact	What options do you have to move forward—what is a commitment
Evaluate	What went well—what do you want to do the next time

Powerful questions are tailored depending on needs. These questions can be used for self-reflection, with others, or in teams. These questions are not jaw-droppingly original, but they have been tested in real life by thousands of leaders and coaches.

Purpose	Why do you do what you do—what do you want to be known for
Discovery	What is your intention—what do you have agency over
Clarity	What does this mean for you—what does your intuition say
Reflection	What is working for you/the team—what is resonating—what is not working
Reframe	What is the impact if things remain the same—what is another way to see this
Support	How can you ask for what you need—what might help you feel safer right now
Regulate	How can you take care of yourself right now—what will you say no to
Engagement	Might you be willing to…—what would encourage you to…
Action	What is one step you will commit to—what excites you to move forward

Active Listening

Most people are not as great listeners as they think they are.[1] To actively listen, you must activate different parts of your brain and body to attune to the message content and to emotional responses, body language, tone, pitch, and pace.[2] It is one thing to listen to what you want to hear and another to listen to the other person's intention. Active listening requires you to consider whether the recipient gets what you intended to say and signal back to ensure mutual understanding.[3]

There are different levels of listening; one is not necessarily better than another. Wisdom comes from knowing which to employ given a particular situation. In an emergency, you may need to ignore certain noises to focus and respond quickly. When troubleshooting a technical issue, selective listening may be the most productive. Silence awareness warrants deep listening.

Listening	Behavior	Purpose
Ignoring	Not listening	Concentrate on something else
Pretending	Demonstrating listening behaviors without listening	Protect self
Selective	Listening for words/phrases	Discover relevant information
Attentive	Listening for words from their perspective	Understand and engage
Empathic	Listening for words, emotions, and body language from their perspective	Understand and empathize
Active Constructive	Centering the other person while guiding the conversation	Support the other person to awareness and/or action

Active listening helps you to check whether you are making unfounded assumptions before they unnecessarily snowball into larger issues. Developed by Chris Argyris and Donald Schon[4] and later popularized by Peter Senge,[5] the left-hand column technique offers a framework to question your assumptions about what you hear, or at least, think you hear.

What you think they were thinking	What you were thinking	What was said
I could care less about what you think.	I don't think you're going to do anything with it.	"I appreciate your feedback."
I am surprised you didn't screw up like you usually do.	I have no clue what I'm doing and now you know.	"You did great at the meeting."

The Art of Improvisation

What do Proctor & Gamble, Pixar, and Prudential have in common? Yes, they begin with the letter 'p' and these companies have brought into their boardrooms and teams another 'p'—play—in the form of improvisation or 'improv' to help boost innovation, creativity, communication, and trust. Improv invites purposeful play and structured vulnerability, which have multiple benefits, including positive group dynamics, and creativity.[6]

The great news is that MBA and graduate programs are increasingly incorporating the teaching of improv.[7] After all, as a leader, you must be agile to strategize and act. Harvard Business School Professor Francesca Gino found that leaders who adopt improv skills are better at managing power dynamics through listening, adaptability, and open-mindedness. Improvisers are skilled in focusing on the here and now to create the new.[8] The scene is literally being built as they go, so they cannot worry too far ahead or ruminate too far in the past. Indeed, the rules of improv apply to compassionate leadership and Gary Pisano's five key principles of innovation.[9]

Five "things" of innovation, improv, and compassionate leadership[10]

	Innovation	Improv	Compassionate leadership
1. Curiosity	Tolerance for failure does not equate to incompetence.	Test out scenes and characters. Select talent.	Experiment. Celebrate mistakes.
2. Child's mind	Willingness to experiment with discipline.	Bring a fresh approach while following "rules."	Prototype and iterate. Set guardrails.
3. Safety	Psychological safety for candor.	Accept and build. Offer feedback to improve.	Encourage healthy candor and conflict.
4. Paradox	Collaboration with individual accountability.	Cocreate scenes by "gifting" and owning parts.	Pause. Share point of view. Be open.
5. Play	Flat, strong leadership.	Guide with shared ownership.	Empower others to self-manage.

While there is no "right" way to leadership, there are some core characteristics and mindsets that are particularly conducive to effective leadership. The four fundamental leadership mindsets posed by Robert Quinn share many of the same principles as improv (Quinn 2005).[11]

Fundamental state of leadership and fundamental state of improv[12]

Fundamental state of leadership (Quinn 2005)	Fundamental state of improv (Chiu 2022a)
Results-centered; open to nonexistent possibilities	Create something out of nothing at all
Internally directed; willing to initiate productive conflict	Find the absurd; call out the obstacle; seek tension; lean into the discomfort
Other-focused; committed to the collective good	Focus on the bigger picture, outcome, and scene partner, aka It's Not About You
Externally directed; willing to depart from the routine	Do the unexpected; invite perspectives; bend rules of "should-would-could"

In short, you can enhance your effectiveness by building your improvisation skillset.

The Ripple Effect

Whatever your role is, you lead every day through your actions and behaviors. Your actions have a ripple effect on all with whom you directly engage and those whom you indirectly impact. Even a small individual action may lead to profound change. As Drew Dudley highlighted, leadership is a series of small moments, or what he calls "lollipop leadership," "special moment[s] where one individual positively shapes another person's life but may not realize his or her impact."[13] Becoming more aware of the small and big moments position you to leave teams, organizations, and the world better than you found them. Continue reflecting on and investigating how to integrate the themes you explored in this playbook with greater compassion, clarity, and courage. And hopefully, to spur continued growth.

Notes

Introduction

1. Chiu, "The Laughing Buddha: The Education of Compassionate Leaders Through Improvisational Play."
2. International Coaching Federation, "Read About ICF."
3. Keil, "Coaching for Leaders."; Halliwell, Mitchell, and Boyle, "Leadership Effectiveness Through Coaching," e0294953.
4. DiGirolamo and Tkach, "An Exploration of Managers and Leaders Using Coaching Skills," 195–218.
5. George and Clayton, "Successful Leaders Are Great Coaches."; Ibarra, "The Leader as Coach."
6. Gavin, "Authentic Leadership."
7. Jensen and Luthans, "Entrepreneurs as Authentic Leaders," 646–666.
8. Tjan, "How Leaders Become Self-Aware."
9. Salovey and Mayer, "Emotional Intelligence," 185–211; Goleman, *The Emotionally Intelligent Leader*; Goleman, Boyatzis, and McKee, "Primal Leadership: Realizing the Power of Emotional Intelligence," 40–0392; Goleman, *Working With Emotional Intelligence*; Landry, "How to Develop Emotional Intelligence Skills."
10. Coronado-Maldonado and Benítez-Márquez, "Emotional Intelligence, Leadership, and Work Teams: A Hybrid Literature Review," e20356; Hougaard, "Power Can Corrupt Leaders. Compassion Can Save Them."
11. Passmore, "Leading With Compassion."; Hougaard, "Effective Leaders Move Beyond Empathy to Compassion."
12. Chiu, "Leading With a Compassion Strategy."
13. Chiu, "Leading With a Compassion Strategy: Centeredness."
14. Chiu, "Leading With a Compassion Strategy: Courage."
15. Chiu, "Leading With a Compassion Strategy: Curiosity."

Chapter 1

1. Markway and Ampel, *The Self Confidence Workbook.*
2. Bennis and Thomas, "Crucibles of Leadership," *Ibid.*
3. George, *Discover Your True North.*
4. Harvard Business Review Analytic Services, "The Business Case for Purpose."; Bailey et al., CIPD.
5. Craig, "From Purpose to Impact."
6. Sinek, *Start With Why.*
7. Abuhamdeh, "Investigating the 'Flow' Experience,"
8. Kotler, "Create a Work Environment That Fosters Flow."
9. Mumford, *The Mindful Athlete.*
10. Perlow, "Stop the Meeting Madness,"
11. Carrier et al., "Causes, Effects, and Practicalities of Everyday Multi-tasking," 64–78.
12. Madore and Wagner, "Multicosts of Multitasking."
13. Peterson, Maier, and Seligman, "Learned Helplessness,"
14. Domenico and Ryan, "The Emerging Neuroscience of Intrinsic Motivation,"
15. Core Strengths, *Corestrength.com.*
16. Asplund and Hickman, *Gallup.Com.*
17. Dubord and Forest, "Focusing on Strengths or Weaknesses?"
18. Kaplan, "Stop Overdoing Your Strengths."
19. Proyer et al, "Strengths-based Positive Psychology Interventions."
20. Seligman et al, "Positive Psychology Progress," 410–21.
21. Sakulku and Alexander, "The Impostor Phenomenon." 75–97.
22. Robson, *New Scientist.*
23. National Scientific Council on the Developing Child, "Supportive Relationships and Active Skill-Building Strengthen the Foundations of Resilience."
24. Mitamura, Reuman, and Tugade, *Resilience,* 5529–5531.
25. Cohn et al., "Happiness Unpacked," 361–368.
26. Aristotle, "The Nicomachean Ethics of Aristotle."
27. Kożusznik, Peiró and Soriano, "Daily Eudaimonic Well-being as a Predictor of Daily Performance."

28. Deci and Ryan, "Hedonia, Eudaimonia, and Well-being," 1–11.
29. Kuhn et al., "The Own and Social Effects of an Unexpected Income Shock."
30. Armenta et al., "Is Lasting Change Possible?" 57–74.
31. Mogi, *The Little Book of Ikigai.*
32. Pacheco, Sleep Foundation
33. Pink, *When: The Scientific Secrets of Perfect Timing.*
34. Mayer-Schonberger and Oberlechner, "Through Their Own Words."
35. Nardon and Hari, "Sensemaking Through Metaphors."
36. Jacobs and Heracleous, "Constructing Shared Understanding," 207–226.
37. Norcross and Vangarelli, "The Resolution Solution," 127–134.
38. Berkman, "The Neuroscience of Goals and Behavior Change," 28–44.
39. Oscarsson, et al., "A Large-Scale Experiment on New Year's Resolutions," e0234097.
40. Pally, *The Predicting Brain,* 193–217.
41. Ranganathan et al., "From Mental Power to Muscle Power—Gaining Strength by Using the Mind," 944–956
42. Latham and Locke, "New Developments in and Directions for Goal-Setting Research," 290–300.
43. Nawaz et al., "Going Deep Into a Leader's Integrity," 845–863
44. Dass et al., "A Study of the Antecedents of Slogan Liking," 2504–2511.
45. Gorbatov, Khapova, and Lysova, "Personal Branding."
46. Avery, "A New Approach to Building Your Personal Brand."

Chapter 2

1. Hale, *The Performance Consultant's Fieldbook.*
2. Alagaraja and Shuck, "Exploring Organizational Alignment-Employee Engagement Linkages and Impact on Individual Performance," 17–37.
3. Roberts, "How to Play to Your Strengths."
4. Friedman et al., "Chronic Stress Alters Striosome-Circuit Dynamics, Leading to Aberrant Decision-Making," 1191–1205.

5. Chang, 2014. "How to Make Hard Choices."

6. Cross, "The Secret to Building Resilience."

7. Kram and Higgins, "A New Mindset on Mentoring: Creating Developmental Networks at Work."

8. Stelter, "Want to Advance in Your Career? Build Your Own Board of Directors."

9. Granovetter, "The Strength of Weak Ties," 1360-1380.

10. Macintosh and Stevens, "Personality, Motives, and Conflict Strategies in Everyday Service Encounters," 112–131.

11. Thomas and Kilmann, "Thomas-Kilmann Conflict Mode Instrument."

12. Rond, "Conflict Keeps Teams at the Top of Their Game."

13. Jehn et al., "The Effects of Conflict Types, Dimensions, and Emergent States on Group Outcomes," 465–495.

14. Kumar, "A Framework for Rethinking Leadership for the Long Run."

15. Lu, Fang, and Qiu, "Rejecters Overestimate the Negative Consequences They Will Face From Refusal," 280–291.

16. Wepfer et al., "Work-Life Boundaries and Well-Being: Does Work-to-Life Integration Impair Well-Being Through Lack of Recovery?" 727–740.

17. Ury, *The Power of a Positive No.*

18. Urrila, "From Personal Wellbeing to Relationships: A Systematic Review on the Impact of Mindfulness Interventions and Practices on Leaders," 100837.

19. Chiu, "Leading With a Compassion Strategy: Centeredness."

20. Porges, "Polyvagal Theory: A Science of Safety."

21. Govindarajan, *The Three-Box Solution: A Strategy for Leading Innovation.*

22. Kanter, "Zoom in, Zoom Out," 112-116, 131.

23. Burnes, "The Origins of Lewin's Three-Step Model of Change," 32–59.

24. Yahya and Sukmayadi, "A Review of Cognitive Dissonance Theory and Its Relevance to Current Social Issues."

25. Am et al., "Innovation in a Crisis: Why It Is More Critical Than Ever."

26. Tyrrell et al., "Kubler-Ross Stages of Dying and Subsequent Models of Grief."

27. Bandura, "Self-Efficacy: Toward a Unifying Theory of Behavioral Change," 191–215; Schwarzer and Warner, "Perceived Self-Efficacy

and Its Relationship to Resilience," 139–150.; Lippke, *Self-Efficacy Theory*, 4722–4727; Seligman, *Learned Optimism*.

28. Kronborg et al., "Control and Resilience: The Importance of an Internal Focus to Maintain Resilience in Academically Able Students," 59–74.

29. Kotter, *A Sense of Urgency*.

30. Keller and Schaninger, "Getting Personal About Change."

31. Centola, "The Truth About Behavioral Change."; Centola, et al., "Experimental *Evidence* for Tipping Points in Social Convention," 1116–1119.

32. Hatfield, Cacioppo, and Rapson, "Emotional Contagion," 96–100.

33. Barsade, "The Ripple Effect: Emotional Contagion and Its Influence on Group Behavior," 644–675; Barsade and Gibson, "Why Does Affect Matter in Organizations?" 36–59.;

34. Barsade, "The Contagion We Can Control."

35. Rosenberg and Chopra, *Nonviolent Communication: A Language of Life: Life-Changing Tools for Healthy Relationships*.

36. Nosek, "Nonviolent Communication: A Dialogical Retrieval of the Ethic of Authenticity," 829–837.

37. Cheung et al., "Reliability and Validity of a Novel Measure of Nonviolent Communication Behaviors," 790–797.

38. Erickson, "Communication in a Crisis and the Importance of Authenticity and Transparency," 476–483.

39. Chiu, "Leading With a Compassion Strategy: Courage."

40. Ladders Research, "Career Strategy: 88% of Professionals Say 'Managing up' Means Career Success."

41. Rousmaniere, "What Everyone Should Know About Managing Up."

42. Doherty, "How to Effectively Manage Up," 99–106.

43. Gabarro and Kotter, "Managing Your Boss."

44. Goleman, "Leadership That Gets Results."

45. Gnepp et al., "The Future of Feedback: Motivating Performance Improvement Through Future-focused Feedback," e0234444.

46. Berinato, "Research: Negative Feedback Rarely Helps People Improve."; Buckingham, "Why Feedback Rarely Does What It's Meant To."

47. Phoel, "Feedback That Works."; Chappelow, "What Good Feedback Really Looks Like."

Chapter 3

1. Maister, Green, and Galford, *The Trusted Advisor*.

2. Kenrick et al., "Renovating the Pyramid of Needs," 292–314; Porges, "Polyvagal Theory: A Science of Safety."

3. Newman, Donohue, and Eva, "Psychological Safety: A Systematic Review of the Literature," 521–535.

4. Loignon and Wormington, "Psychologically Safe for Some, but Not All? The Downsides of Assuming Shared Psychological Safety Among Senior Leadership Teams."

5. Clark, *The 4 Stages of Psychological Safety*; Clark, "How a CEO Can Create Psychological Safety in the Room."

6. Clark, *The 4 Stages of Psychological Safety*.

7. Alwood, "Landmark Workplace Study Reveals Crisis of Accountability."

8. Carucci, "How to Actually Encourage Employee Accountability."

9. Edmondson, *The Fearless Organization*.

10. Rousseau, "Psychological and Implied Contracts in Organizations," 121–139.

11. PricewaterhouseCoopers, "Global Culture Survey 2021 Report."

12. Ibid.

13. Norton and Sussman, "Team Charters: Theoretical Foundations and Practical Implications for Quality and Performance," 7–17.

14. Pratt, "Collective Intelligence," 303–309.

15. Green, "Testing and Quantifying Collective Intelligence."

16. Woolley et al., "Evidence for a Collective Intelligence Factor in the Performance of Human Groups," 686–688.

17. Felfernig et al., "Biases in Group Decisions," 153–163.

18. Gander, Gaitzsch, and Ruch, "The Relationships of Team Role- and Character Strengths-Balance With Individual and Team-Level Satisfaction and Performance."

19. VIA Institute on Character, "Team Report."

20. Gallup, Inc., "How to Create a Strengths-Based Culture."

21. Van Woerkom, Meyers, and Bakker, "Considering Strengths Use in Organizations as a Multilevel Construct," 100767.

22. Mlodinow, *Subliminal: How Your Unconscious Mind Rules Your Behavior*.

23. Förderer and Unkelbach, "Attribute Conditioning: Changing Attribute-assessments Through Mere Pairings," 144–64.

24. Jones, "Unconscious Bias," 74–78; Phillips-Wren, Power, and Mora, "Cognitive Bias, Decision Styles, and Risk Attitudes in Decision Making and DSS," 63–66.

25. Samide and Ritchey, "Reframing the Past: Role of Memory Processes in Emotion Regulation," 848–857.

26. Kouzes, "To Lead, Create a Shared Vision."

27. Mahmood and Rehman, "Impact of Effective Vision Attributes on Employee Satisfaction."

28. Tichy, *The Leadership Engine.*

29. Gothelf, "Storytelling Can Make or Break Your Leadership."

30. Bonchek, "How to Build a Strategic Narrative."

31. Duarte, "The Secret Structure of Great Talks."

32. Ready, "The Power of a Clear Leadership Narrative."

33. Am et al., "Innovation in a Crisis: Why It Is More Critical Than Ever."

34. Ku, Wang, and Galinsky, "The Promise and Perversity of Perspective-Taking in Organizations," 79–102.

35. Chamorro-Premuzic, "Does Diversity Actually Increase Creativity?"

36. de Bono, *Lateral Thinking.*

37. Liu, Xu, and Zhang, "Thriving at Work," 347–366.

38. Sheppard and Anfield, "The Urgent Need for Sophisticated Leadership."

39. Pew Research Center, "Most Americans Say Coronavirus Outbreak Has Impacted Their Lives."; Ramalingam, "5 Principles to Guide Adaptive Leadership."

40. Heifetz and Linsky, *Leadership on the Line.*

41. Ryan and Deci, "Self-Determination Theory and the Facilitation of Intrinsic Motivation, Social Development, and Well-being.," 68–78.

42. Gehlbach and Mu, "How We Understand Others: A Theory of How Social Perspective Taking Unfolds," 282–302.

43. Kraus, Côté, and Keltner, "Social Class, Contextualism, and Empathic Accuracy," 1716–1723.

44. Taylor, "Persuading Your Team to Embrace Change."

45. Park and Park, "How Can Employees Adapt to Change? Clarifying the Adaptive Performance Concepts."

46. Miller, "5 Steps in the Change Management Process."

47. Onderick-Harvey, "5 Ways to Help Your Team Be Open to Change."

48. Mládková, "Leadership and Storytelling," 83–90; Peterson, "The Science Behind the Art of Storytelling."; Martinez-Conde et al., "The Storytelling Brain," 8285–8290.

49. Zak, "Why Inspiring Stories Make Us React," 2.

50. Zak, *The Moral Molecule.*

Retrospection

1. Zenger and Folkman, "What Great Listeners Actually Do."

2. Gallo, "What Is Active Listening?"

3. Tennant, Butler, and Long, "Active Listening."

4. Argyris and Schön, *Theory in Practice: Increasing Professional Effectiveness.*

5. Senge, *The Fifth Discipline.*

6. Chiu, "The Laughing Buddha."

7. Flucht, "When the Art of the Deal Includes Improv Training."; Gino, "Using Improv to Unite Your Team."

8. Ibid.

9. Pisano, "The Hard Truth about Innovative Cultures."

10. Chiu, *Action Compassion.*

11. Quinn, "Moments of Greatness: Entering the Fundamental State of Leadership," 74-83, 191.

12. Chiu, *Action Compassion.*

13. Dudley, "Leading With Lollipops."

References

Abuhamdeh, Sami. February 2020. "Investigating the 'Flow' Experience: Key Conceptual and Operational Issues." *Frontiers in Psychology* 11 (158). https://doi.org/10.3389/fpsyg.2020.00158.

Alagaraja, Meera, and Brad Shuck. January 2015. "Exploring Organizational Alignment-Employee Engagement Linkages and Impact on Individual Performance." *Human Resource Development Review* 14 (1): 17–37. https://doi.org/10.1177/1534484314549455.

Alwood, Brent. 2024. "Landmark Workplace Study Reveals Crisis of Accountability." *Culture Partners*, January. https://culturepartners.com/insights/landmark-workplace-study-reveals-crisis-of-accountability/.

Am, Jordan Bar, Laura Furstenthal, Felicitas Jorge, and Erik Roth. 2020. "Innovation in a Crisis: Why It Is More Critical Than Ever." *McKinsey & Company,* June. www.mckinsey.com/capabilities/strategy-and-corporate-finance/our-insights/innovation-in-a-crisis-why-it-is-more-critical-than-ever.

Argyris, Chris, and Donald A Schön. 1974. *Theory in Practice: Increasing Professional Effectiveness.* 1st ed. San Francisco, California: Jossey-Bass.

Aristotle. 1884. *The Nicomachean Ethics of Aristotle.* London: Paul.

Armenta, Christina, Katherine Jacobs Bao, Sonja Lyubomirsky, and Kennon M. Sheldon. July 2014. "Is Lasting Change Possible? Lessons From the Hedonic Adaptation Prevention Model." *Stability of Happiness*, 57–74. https://doi.org/10.1016/b978-0-12-411478-4.00004-7.

Asplund, Jim, and Adam Hickman. 2021. "What We Learned From 25 Million CliftonStrengths Assessments." *GallupStrengths*, April. www.gallup.com/cliftonstrengths/en/344669/learned-million-cliftonstrengths-assessments.aspx.

Avery, Jill. 2023. "A New Approach to Building Your Personal Brand." *Harvard Business Review*, July. https://hbr.org/2023/05/a-new-approach-to-building-your-personal-brand.

Bailey, C., Shantz, A., Brione, P., Yarlagadda, R., CIPD, YouGov, & Oxford University. *Purposeful Leadership: What Is It, What Causes It, and Does It Matter? CIPD,* 2017. www.cipd.org/globalassets/media/knowledge/knowledge-hub/reports/purposeful-leadership_2017-technical-report_tcm18-24076.pdf.

Bandura, Albert. January 1977. "Self-efficacy: Toward a Unifying Theory of Behavioral Change." *Psychological Review* 84 (2): 191–215. https://doi.org/10.1037/0033-295x.84.2.191.

Barsade, Sigal G. December 2002. "The Ripple Effect: Emotional Contagion and Its Influence on Group Behavior." *Administrative Science Quarterly* 47 (4): 644–675. https://doi.org/10.2307/3094912.

Barsade, Sigal. 2021. "The Contagion We Can Control." *Harvard Business Review*, February. https://hbr.org/2020/03/the-contagion-we-can-control.

Barsade, Sigal G., and Donald E. Gibson. February 2007. "Why Does Affect Matter in Organizations?" *the Academy of Management Perspectives/Academy of Management Perspectives* 21 (1): 36–59. https://doi.org/10.5465/amp.2007.24286163.

Bennis, Warren, and Robert J. Thomas. 2002. "Crucibles of Leadership." *Harvard Business Review*, June. https://hbr.org/2002/09/crucibles-of-leadership.

Berinato, Scott. 2020. "Research: Negative Feedback Rarely Helps People Improve." *Harvard Business Review*, November. https://hbr.org/2018/01/negative-feedback-rarely-leads-to-improvement.

Berkman, Elliot T. March 2018. "The Neuroscience of Goals and Behavior Change." *Consulting Psychology Journal* 70, no. 1: 28–44. https://doi.org/10.1037/cpb0000094.

Bonchek, Mark. 2016. "How to Build a Strategic Narrative." *Harvard Business Review*, July. https://hbr.org/2016/03/how-to-build-a-strategic-narrative.

Buckingham, Marcus. 2024. "Why Feedback Rarely Does What It's Meant To." *Harvard Business Review*, February. https://hbr.org/2019/03/the-feedback-fallacy.

Burnes, Bernard. December 2019. "The Origins of Lewin's Three-Step Model of Change." *Journal of Applied Behavioral Science* no. 1: 32–59. https://doi.org/10.1177/0021886319892685.

Carrier, L. Mark, Larry D. Rosen, Nancy A. Cheever, and Alex F. Lim. March 2015. "Causes, Effects, and Practicalities of Everyday Multitasking." *Developmental Review* 35: 64–78. https://doi.org/10.1016/j.dr.2014.12.005.

Carucci, Ron. 2020. "How to Actually Encourage Employee Accountability." *Harvard Business Review*, November. https://hbr.org/2020/11/how-to-actually-encourage-employee-accountability.

Centola, Damon, Joshua Becker, Devon Brackbill, and Andrea Baronchelli. June 2018. "Experimental Evidence for Tipping Points in Social Convention." *Science* 360 (6393): 1116–1119. https://doi.org/10.1126/science.aas8827.

Centola, Damon. 2018. "The Truth About Behavioral Change." *MIT Sloan Management Review*, November. https://ndg.asc.upenn.edu/wp-content/uploads/2018/11/The-Truth-About-Behavioral-Change.pdf.

Chamorro-Premuzic, Tomas. 2017; "Does Diversity Actually Increase Creativity?" *Harvard Business Review*, June. https://hbr.org/2017/06/does-diversity-actually-increase-creativity.

Chang, Ruth. 2014. "How to Make Hard Choices." TEDSalon NY, May. Video, 14:27. www.ted.com/talks/ruth_chang_how_to_make_hard_choices.

Chappelow, Craig. 2019. "What Good Feedback Really Looks Like." *Harvard Business Review*, June. https://hbr.org/2019/05/what-good-feedback-really-looks-like.

Cheung, Cherry T.Y., Clement Man-Him Cheng, Stanley Kam Ki Lam, Henry Wai-Hang Ling, Kim Ling Lau, Suet Lin Hung, and Hong Wang Fung. September 2022. "Reliability and Validity of a Novel Measure of Nonviolent Communication Behaviors." *Research on Social Work Practice* 33, no. 7: 790–797. https://doi.org/10.1177/10497315221128595.

Chiu, Belinda. 2022. Leading With a Compassion Strategy: Centeredness." *Tuck Executive Education*, July. https://exec.tuck.dartmouth.edu/news-insights/compassion-strategy-centeredness.

Chiu, Belinda. 2022a. *Action Compassion: Improv Playbook for Those Who Care.* NH: Hummingbirdrcc.

Chiu, Belinda. 2022b. Leading With a Compassion Strategy." *Tuck Executive Education at Dartmouth*, May. https://exec.tuck.dartmouth.edu/news-insights/leading-with-a-compassion-strategy/.

Chiu, Belinda. 2022c. Leading With a Compassion Strategy: Courage." *Tuck Executive Education*, September. https://exec.tuck.dartmouth.edu/news-insights/compassion-strategy-courage/.

Chiu, Belinda. 2022. Leading With a Compassion Strategy: Curiosity." *Tuck Executive Education*, October. https://exec.tuck.dartmouth.edu/news-insights/compassion-strategy-curiosity.

Chiu, Belinda. 2024. The Laughing Buddha: The Education of Compassionate Leaders Through Improvisational Play, *Journal of Contemplative and Holistic Education* 2, no. 2. https://scholarworks.bgsu.edu/jche/vol2/iss2/3/.

Clark, Timothy R. 2020. *The 4 Stages of Psychological Safety: Defining the Path to Inclusion and Innovation.* Berrett-Koehler Publishers.

Clark, Timothy R. 2023. "How a CEO Can Create Psychological Safety in the Room." *Harvard Business Review*, January. https://hbr.org/2023/01/how-a-ceo-can-create-psychological-safety-in-the-room.

Cohn, Michael A., Barbara L. Fredrickson, Stephanie L. Brown, Joseph A. Mikels, and Anne M. Conway. June 2009. "Happiness Unpacked: Positive Emotions Increase Life Satisfaction by Building Resilience." *Emotion* 9 (3): 361–368. https://doi.org/10.1037/a0015952.

Core Strengths. n.d. "Strength Deployment Inventory 2.0." *Corestrengths.com.* www.corestrengths.com/products/assessment/.

Coronado-Maldonado, Isabel, and María-Dolores Benítez-Márquez. October 2023. "Emotional Intelligence, Leadership, and Work Teams: A Hybrid Literature Review." *Heliyon* 9 (10): e20356. https://doi.org/10.1016/j.heliyon.2023.e20356.

Craig, Nick. 2021. "From Purpose to Impact." *Harvard Business Review*, September. https://hbr.org/2014/05/from-purpose-to-impact.

Cross, Rob. 2021. "The Secret to Building Resilience." *Harvard Business Review*, September. https://hbr.org/2021/01/the-secret-to-building-resilience.

Dass, Mayuch, Chiranjeev Kohli, Piyush Kumar, and Sunil Thomas. December 2014. "A Study of the Antecedents of Slogan Liking." *Journal of Business Research* 67 (12): 2504–2511. https://doi.org/10.1016/j.jbusres.2014.05.004.

De Bono, Edward. 2014. *Lateral Thinking: An Introduction*. Random House.

De Rond, Mark. 2017. "Conflict Keeps Teams at the Top of Their Game." *Harvard Business Review*, May. https://hbr.org/2012/07/conflict-keeps-teams-at-the-to.

Deci, Edward L., and Richard M. Ryan. November 2006. "Hedonia, Eudaimonia, and Well-being: An Introduction." *Journal of Happiness Studies* 9 (1): 1–11. https://doi.org/10.1007/s10902-006-9018-1.

Di Domenico, Stefano I. and Richard M. Ryan. March 2017. "The Emerging Neuroscience of Intrinsic Motivation: A New Frontier in Self-Determination Research." *Frontiers in Human Neuroscience* 11. https://doi.org/10.3389/fnhum.2017.00145.

DiGirolamo, Joel A., and J. Thomas Tkach. September 2019. "An Exploration of Managers and Leaders Using Coaching Skills." *Consulting Psychology Journal* 71 (3), 195–218. https://doi.org/10.1037/cpb0000138.

Doherty, Gerard M. July 2019. "How to Effectively Manage Up." In *Success in Academic Surgery*, 99–106. https://doi.org/10.1007/978-3-030-19854-1_10.

Duarte, Nancy. 2011. "The Secret Structure of Great Talks." TEDxEast. Video, 18:00, November. www.ted.com/talks/nancy_duarte_the_secret_structure_of_great_talks.

Dubord, Marc-Antoine Gradito, and Jacques Forest. September 2022. "Focusing on Strengths or Weaknesses? Using Self-Determination Theory to Explain Why a Strengths-Based Approach Has More Impact on Optimal Functioning Than Deficit Correction." *International Journal of Applied Positive Psychology*. https://doi.org/10.1007/s41042-022-00079-x.

Dudley, Drew. 2010. "Leading With Lollipops." TEDx Toronto. Video, 6:00, September. www.youtube.com/watch?v=hVCBrkrFrBE.

Edmondson, Amy C. 2018. *The Fearless Organization: Creating Psychological Safety in the Workplace for Learning, Innovation, and Growth*. John Wiley & Sons.

Erickson, Sue. May 2021. "Communication in a Crisis and the Importance of Authenticity and Transparency." *Journal of Library Administration* 61 (4): 476–83. https://doi.org/10.1080/01930826.2021.1906556.

Felfernig, Alexander, Müslüm Atas, Martin Stettinger, Thi Ngoc Trang Tran, and Gerhard Leitner. September 2023. "Biases in Group Decisions." In *Signals and Communication Technology*, 153–163. https://doi.org/10.1007/978-3-031-44943-7_8.

Flucht, Julia. 2012. "When the Art of the Deal Includes Improv Training." *NPR*, December. www.npr.org/2012/12/05/166484466/it-s-improv-night-at-business-school.

Förderer, Sabine, and Christian Unkelbach. January 2015. "Attribute Conditioning: Changing Attribute-Assessments Through Mere Pairings." *Quarterly Journal of Experimental Psychology* 68 (1): 144–164. https://doi.org/10.1080/17470218.2014.939667.

Friedman, Alexander, Daigo Homma, Bernard Bloem, Leif G. Gibb, Ken-Ichi Amemori, Dan Hu, Sebastien Delcasso, et al. November 2017. "Chronic Stress Alters Striosome-Circuit Dynamics, Leading to Aberrant Decision-Making." *Cell* 171 (5): 1191–1205.e28. https://doi.org/10.1016/j.cell.2017.10.017.

Gabarro, John J., and John P. Kotter. 2005. "Managing Your Boss." *Harvard Business Review*, January. https://hbr.org/2005/01/managing-your-boss.

Gallo, Amy. 2024. "What Is Active Listening?" *Harvard Business Review*, January. https://hbr.org/2024/01/what-is-active-listening.

Gallup, Inc. 2022. "How to Create a Strengths-Based Culture." *Gallup.com*, October. www.gallup.com/cliftonstrengths/en/290903/how-to-create-strengths-based-company-culture.aspx.

Gander, Fabian, Ines Gaitzsch, and Willibald Ruch. November 2020. "The Relationships of Team Role- and Character Strengths-Balance With Individual and Team-Level Satisfaction and Performance." *Frontiers in Psychology* 11. https://doi.org/10.3389/fpsyg.2020.566222.

Gavin, Matt. 2019. "Authentic Leadership: What It Is & Why It's Important." *Business Insights Blog*, December. https://online.hbs.edu/blog/post/authentic-leadership.

Gehlbach, Hunter, and Nan Mu. January 2023. "How We Understand Others: A Theory of How Social Perspective Taking Unfolds." *Review of General Psychology* 27 (03): 282–302. https://doi.org/10.1177/10892680231152595.

George, Bill. 2015. *Discover Your True North*. John Wiley & Sons.

George, Bill and Zach Clayton. 2022. "Successful Leaders Are Great Coaches." *Harvard Business Review*, October. https://hbr.org/2022/10/successful-leaders-are-great-coaches.

Gino, Francesca. 2019. "Using Improv to Unite Your Team." *Harvard Business Review*, May. https://hbr.org/2019/05/using-improv-to-unite-your-team.

Gnepp, Jackie, Joshua Klayman, Ian O. Williamson, and Sema Barlas. June 2020. "The Future of Feedback: Motivating Performance Improvement Through Future-focused Feedback." *PloS One* 15 (6): e0234444. https://doi.org/10.1371/journal.pone.0234444.

Goleman, Daniel. 2019. *The Emotionally Intelligent Leader*. MA: Harvard Business Press.

Goleman, Daniel. 2000. "Leadership That Gets Results." *Harvard Business Review*, March. https://hbr.org/2000/03/leadership-that-gets-results.

Goleman, Daniel. 2011. *Working With Emotional Intelligence*. Bantam.

Goleman, Daniel, Richard Boyatzis, and Annie McKee. September 2002. "Primal Leadership: Realizing the Power of Emotional Intelligence." *Choice Reviews Online* 40 (01): 40–0392. https://doi.org/10.5860/choice.40-0392.

Gothelf, Jeff. 2021. "Storytelling Can Make or Break Your Leadership." *Harvard Business Review*, November. https://hbr.org/2020/10/storytelling-can-make-or-break-your-leadership.

Govindarajan, Vijay. 2016. *The Three-Box Solution: A Strategy for Leading Innovation*. MA: Harvard Business Review Press.

Granovetter, Mark S. May 1973. "The Strength of Weak Ties." *American Journal of Sociology* 78 (6): 1360–1380. www.jstor.org/stable/2776392.

Green, Ben. 2015. "Testing and Quantifying Collective Intelligence." *Collective Intelligence*. https://scholar.harvard.edu/sites/scholar.harvard.edu/files/bgreen/files/ci2015-paper.pdf.

Hale, Judith. 2012. *The Performance Consultant's Fieldbook: Tools and Techniques for Improving Organizations and People*. John Wiley & Sons.

Halliwell, Peter R., Rebecca J. Mitchell, and Brendan Boyle. December 2023. "Leadership Effectiveness Through Coaching: Authentic and Change-Oriented Leadership." *PloS One* 18 (12): e0294953. https://doi.org/10.1371/journal.pone.0294953.

Harvard Business Review Analytic Services. April 2016. "The Business Case for Purpose." *Harvard Business*, April. https://assets.ey.com/content/dam/ey-sites/ey-com/en_gl/topics/digital/ey-the-business-case-for-purpose.pdf.

Hatfield, Elaine, John T. Cacioppo, and Richard L. Rapson. June 1993. "Emotional Contagion." *Current Directions in Psychological Science* 2 (3): 96–100. https://doi.org/10.1111/1467-8721.ep10770953.

Heifetz, Ronald Abadian, and Martin Linsky. 2002. *Leadership on the Line: Staying Alive Through the Dangers of Leading*. Harvard Business Press.

Hougaard, Rasmus. 2018. "Power Can Corrupt Leaders. Compassion Can Save Them." *Harvard Business Review*, February. https://hbr.org/2018/02/power-can-corrupt-leaders-compassion-can-save-them.

Hougaard, Rasmus. 2021. "Effective Leaders Move Beyond Empathy to Compassion." *Harvard Business Review*, December. https://hbr.org/2021/12/connect-with-empathy-but-lead-with-compassion.

Ibarra, Herminia. 2024. "The Leader as Coach." *Harvard Business Review*, February. https://hbr.org/2019/11/the-leader-as-coach.

International Coaching Federation. 2023. "Read About ICF." *International Coaching Federation*, October. https://coachingfederation.org/about.

Jacobs, Claus D., and Loizos Th. Heracleous. June 2006. "Constructing Shared Understanding." *Journal of Applied Behavioral Science* 42 (2): 207–226. https://doi.org/10.1177/0021886305284895.

Jehn, Karen A., Lindred Greer, Sheen Levine, and Gabriel Szulanski. April 2008. "The Effects of Conflict Types, Dimensions, and Emergent States on Group Outcomes." *Group Decision and Negotiation* 17 (6): 465–495. https://doi.org/10.1007/s10726-008-9107-0.

Jensen, Susan M., and Fred Luthans. December 2006. "Entrepreneurs as Authentic Leaders: Impact on Employees' Attitudes." *Leadership & Organization Development Journal* 27 (8): 646–666. https://doi.org/10.1108/01437730610709273.

Jones, Derek. 2018. "Unconscious Bias." In *BRILL eBooks*, 74–78. https://doi.org/10.1163/9789463511438_014.

Kanter, Rosabeth Moss. March 2011. "Zoom in, Zoom Out." *PubMed* 89 (3): 112–116, 131. https://pubmed.ncbi.nlm.nih.gov/21513265.

Kaplan, Robert E. 2019. "Stop Overdoing Your Strengths." *Harvard Business Review*, January. https://hbr.org/2009/02/stop-overdoing-your-strengths.

Keil, Andrew. 2020. "Coaching for Leaders." *Center for Creative Leadership*, June. www.ccl.org/wp-content/uploads/2020/06/Coaching-for-leaders-center-for-creative-leadership.pdf.

Keller, Scott, and Bill Schaninger. 2019. "Getting Personal About Change." *McKinsey & Company*, August. www.mckinsey.com/capabilities/people-and-organizational-performance/our-insights/getting-personal-about-change.

Kenrick, Douglas T., Vladas Griskevicius, Steven L. Neuberg, and Mark Schaller. May 2010. "Renovating the Pyramid of Needs." *Perspectives on Psychological Science* 5 (3): 292–314. https://doi.org/10.1177/1745691610369469.

Kotler, Steven. 2019. "Create a Work Environment That Fosters Flow." *Harvard Business Review*, October. https://hbr.org/2014/05/create-a-work-environment-that-fosters-flow.

Kotter, John P. 2008. *A Sense of Urgency*. MA: Harvard Business Press.

Kouzes, James M. 2014. "To Lead, Create a Shared Vision." *Harvard Business Review*, August. https://hbr.org/2009/01/to-lead-create-a-shared-vision.

Kożusznik, Małgorzata W., José M. Peiró, and Aida Soriano. April 2019. "Daily Eudaimonic Well-being as a Predictor of Daily Performance: A Dynamic Lens." *PloS One* 14 (4): e0215564. https://doi.org/10.1371/journal.pone.0215564.

Kram, Kathy and Monica Higgins. 2009. "A New Mindset on Mentoring: Creating Developmental Networks at Work." *MIT Sloan Management Review*, April. www.bumc.bu.edu/facdev-medicine/files/2009/12/Kram-Higgins_A-New-Mindset-on-Mentoring.pdf.

Kraus, Michael W., Stéphane Côté, and Dacher Keltner. October 2010. "Social Class, Contextualism, and Empathic Accuracy." *Psychological Science* 21 (11): 1716–1723. https://doi.org/10.1177/0956797610387613.

Kronborg, Leonie, Margaret Plunkett, Nicholas Gamble, and Yvette Kaman. January 2017. "Control and Resilience: The Importance of an Internal Focus to Maintain Resilience in Academically Able Students." *Gifted and Talented International* 32 (1): 59–74. https://doi.org/10.1080/15332276.2018.1435 378.

Ku, Gillian, Cynthia S. Wang, and Adam D. Galinsky. January 2015. "The Promise and Perversity of Perspective-Taking in Organizations." *Research in Organizational Behavior* 35: 79–102. https://doi.org/10.1016/j.riob.2015 .07.003.

Kuhn, Peter J, Peter Kooreman, Adriaan Soetevent, and Arie Kapteyn. 2008. "The Own and Social Effects of an Unexpected Income Shock: Evidence From the Dutch Postcode Lottery." *UC Santa Barbara: Department of Economics, May.* https://escholarship.org/uc/item/07k895v4.

Kumar, Perdeep. 2020. "A Framework for Rethinking Leadership for the Long Run." *Harvard Business Publishing*, July. www.harvardbusiness.org/a-framework-for-rethinking-leadership-for-the-long-run.

Ladders Research. 2020. "Career Strategy: 88% of Professionals Say 'Managing up' Means Career Success." *Ladders*, March. www.theladders.com/career-advice/managing-up-means-career-success-research.

Landry, Lauren. 2019. "How to Develop Emotional Intelligence Skills" *Business Insights Blog*, October. https://online.hbs.edu/blog/post/emotional-intelligence-skills.

Latham, Gary P., and Edwin A. Locke. January 2007. "New Developments in and Directions for Goal-Setting Research." *European Psychologist* 12 (4): 290–300. https://doi.org/10.1027/1016-9040.12.4.290.

Lippke, Sonia. 2020. "Self-Efficacy Theory." In *Springer eBooks* 4722–4727. https://doi.org/10.1007/978-3-319-24612-3_1167.

Liu, Yanjun, Shiyong Xu, and Bainan Zhang. November 2019. "Thriving at Work: How a Paradox Mindset Influences Innovative Work Behavior." *The Journal of Applied Behavioral Science* 56 (3): 347–366. https://doi .org/10.1177/0021886319888267.

Loignon, Andrew, and Stephanie Wormington. January 2022. "Psychologically Safe for Some, but Not All? The Downsides of Assuming Shared Psychological Safety Among Senior Leadership Teams." *Center for Creative Leadership.* https://doi.org/10.35613/ccl.2022.2048.

Lu, Jingyi, Qingwen Fang, and Tian Qiu. June 2023. "Rejecters Overestimate the Negative Consequences They Will Face From Refusal." *Journal of Experimental Psychology. Applied* 29 (2): 280–291. https://doi.org/10.1037/ xap0000457.

Macintosh, Gerrard, and Charles Stevens. April 2008. "Personality, Motives, and Conflict Strategies in Everyday Service Encounters." *the International Journal of Conflict Management/International Journal of Conflict Management* 19 (2): 112–131. https://doi.org/10.1108/10444060810856067.

Madore, Kevin P, and Anthony D Wagner. 2019. "Multicosts of Multitasking." *PubMed*, April. https://pubmed.ncbi.nlm.nih.gov/32206165.

Mahmood, Saqib, and Atiq Ur Rehman. January 2016. "Impact of Effective Vision Attributes on Employee Satisfaction." *International Journal of Economics & Management Sciences* 05 (02): https://doi.org/10.4172/2162-6359.1000315.

Maister, David H., Charles H. Green, and Robert M. Galford. 2000. *The Trusted Advisor*. Simon and Schuster.

Markway, Barbara and Celia Ampel. 2018. *The Self Confidence Workbook*. Althea Press.

Martinez-Conde, Susana, Robert G. Alexander, Deborah Blum, Noah Britton, Barbara K. Lipska, Gregory J. Quirk, Jamy Ian Swiss, Roel M. Willems, and Stephen L. Macknik. October 2019. "The Storytelling Brain: How Neuroscience Stories Help Bridge the Gap Between Research and Society." *The Journal of Neuroscience* 39 (42): 8285–8290. https://doi.org/10.1523/jneurosci.1180-19.2019.

Mayer-Schoenberger, Viktor, and Thomas Oberlechner. January 2002. "Through Their Own Words: Towards a New Understanding of Leadership Through Metaphors." *Social Science Research Network*. https://doi.org/10.2139/ssrn.357542.

Miller, Kelsey. 2020. "5 Critical Steps in the Change Management Process." *Harvard Business School*, March. https://online.hbs.edu/blog/post/change-management-process.

Mitamura, Chelsea, Lillian Reuman, and Michele Tugade. 2014. "Resilience." In *Springer eBooks*, 5529–31. https://doi.org/10.1007/978-94-007-0753-5_2499.

Mládková, Ludmila. April 2013. "Leadership and Storytelling." *Procedia—Social and Behavioral Sciences* 75: 83–90. https://doi.org/10.1016/j.sbspro.2013.04.010.

Mlodinow, Leonard. 2013. *Subliminal: How Your Unconscious Mind Rules Your Behavior*. Vintage.

Mogi, Ken. 2017. *The Little Book of Ikigai: The Secret Japanese way to Live a Happy and Long Life*. UK: Hachette UK.

Mumford, George. 2015. *The Mindful Athlete*. Parallax Press.

Nardon, Luciara, and Amrita Hari. January 2021. "Sensemaking Through Metaphors: The Role of Imaginative Metaphor Elicitation in Constructing New Understandings." *International Journal of Qualitative Methods* 20: 160940692110195. https://doi.org/10.1177/16094069211019589.

National Scientific Council on the Developing Child. May 2015. "Supportive Relationships and Active Skill-Building Strengthen the Foundations of Resilience: Working Paper No. 13." *Center on the Developing Child at Harvard University.* https://developingchild.harvard.edu/wp-content/uploads/2015/05/The-Science-of-Resilience.pdf.

Nawaz, Asif, Faheem Gul Gilal, Khalil Ahmed Channa, and Rukhsana Gul Gilal. December 2023. "Going Deep Into a Leader's Integrity: A Systematic Review and the Way Forward." *European Management Journal* 41 (6): 845–863. https://doi.org/10.1016/j.emj.2022.11.001.

Newman, Alexander, Ross Donohue, and Nathan Eva. September 2017. "Psychological Safety: A Systematic Review of the Literature." *Human Resource Management Review* 27 (3): 521–535. https://doi.org/10.1016/j.hrmr.2017.01.001.

Norcross, John C., and Dominic J. Vangarelli. 1988. "The Resolution Solution: Longitudinal Examination of New Year's Change Attempts." *Journal of Substance Abuse* 1 (2): 127–134. https://doi.org/10.1016/s0899-3289(88)80016-6.

Norton, William I., and Lyle Sussman. January 2009. "Team Charters: Theoretical Foundations and Practical Implications for Quality and Performance." *the Quality Management Journal* 16 (1): 7–17. https://doi.org/10.1080/10686967.2009.11918214.

Nosek, Marcianna. June 2012. "Nonviolent Communication: A Dialogical Retrieval of the Ethic of Authenticity." *Nursing Ethics* 19 (6): 829–837. https://doi.org/10.1177/0969733012447016.

Onderick-Harvey, Edith. 2019. "5 Ways to Help Your Team Be Open to Change." *Harvard Business Review*, April. https://hbr.org/2019/04/5-ways-to-help-your-team-be-open-to-change.

Oscarsson, Martin, Per Carlbring, Gerhard Andersson, and Alexander Rozental. December 2020. "A Large-Scale Experiment on New Year's Resolutions: Approach-oriented Goals Are More Successful Than Avoidance-oriented Goals." *PloS One* 15 (12): e0234097. https://doi.org/10.1371/journal.pone.0234097.

Pacheco, Danielle. 2024. "Chronotypes: Definition, Types, & Effect on Sleep." *Sleep Foundation*, March. www.sleepfoundation.org/how-sleep-works/chronotypes.

Pally, Regina. 2007. "The Predicting Brain: Psychoanalysis and Repeating the Past in the Present." In *Springer eBooks*: 193–217. https://doi.org/10.1007/88-470-0550-7_8.

Park, Sohee, and Sunyoung Park. October 2020. "How Can Employees Adapt to Change? Clarifying the Adaptive Performance Concepts." *Human Resource Development Quarterly* 32 (1). https://doi.org/10.1002/hrdq.21411.

Passmore, Jonathan. 2019. "Leading With Compassion." *HBS* No. IIR214-PDF-

ENG. Boston: Harvard Business School Publishing, April.

Perlow, Leslie A. 2017. "Stop the Meeting Madness." *Harvard Business Review*, July. https://hbr.org/2017/07/stop-the-meeting-madness.

Peterson, Christopher, Steven F Maier, and Martin E P Seligman. 1993. *Learned Helplessness*. https://doi.org/10.1093/oso/9780195044669.001.0001.

Peterson, Lani. 2017. "The Science Behind the Art of Storytelling." *Harvard Business Publishing*, November. www.harvardbusiness.org/the-science-behind-the-art-of-storytelling.

Pew Research Center. 2020. "Most Americans Say Coronavirus Outbreak Has Impacted Their Lives." *Pew Research Center*, March. www.pewsocialtrends.org/2020/03/30/most-americans-say-coronavirus-outbreak-has-impacted-their-lives/.

Phillips-Wren, Gloria, Daniel J. Power, and Manuel Mora. April 2019. "Cognitive Bias, Decision Styles, and Risk Attitudes in Decision Making and DSS." *Journal of Decision Systems* 28 (2): 63–66. https://doi.org/10.1080/12460125.2019.1646509.

Phoel, Cynthia M. 2014. "Feedback That Works." *Harvard Business Review*, July. https://hbr.org/2009/04/feedback-that-works.

Pink, Daniel H. 2018. *When: The Scientific Secrets of Perfect Timing*. Text Publishing.

Pisano, Gary. 2019. "The Hard Truth About Innovative Cultures." *Harvard Business Review*, January. https://hbr.org/2019/01/the-hard-truth-about-innovative-cultures.

Porges, Stephen W. May 2022. "Polyvagal Theory: A Science of Safety." *Frontiers in Integrative Neuroscience* 16. https://doi.org/10.3389/fnint.2022.871227.

Pratt, S.C. 2010. "Collective Intelligence." In *Elsevier eBooks*, 303–309. https://doi.org/10.1016/b978-0-08-045337-8.00352-1.

Proyer, René T., Fabian Gander, Sara Wellenzohn, and Willibald Ruch. April 2015. "Strengths-based Positive Psychology Interventions: A Randomized Placebo-controlled Online Trial on Long-term Effects for a Signature Strengths- Vs. A Lesser Strengths-intervention." *Frontiers in Psychology*. https://doi.org/10.3389/fpsyg.2015.00456.

PricewaterhouseCoopers. 2021."Global Culture Survey 2021 Report." *PwC*. www.pwc.com/gx/en/issues/upskilling/global-culture-survey-2021/global-culture-survey-2021-report.html.

Quinn, Robert E. July 2005. "Moments of Greatness: Entering the Fundamental State of Leadership." *Harvard Business Review* 83 (7): 74–83, 191. https://pubmed.ncbi.nlm.nih.gov/16028818/.

Ramalingam, Ben. 2020. "5 Principles to Guide Adaptive Leadership." *Harvard*

Business Review, September. https://hbr.org/2020/09/5-principles-to-guide-adaptive-leadership.

Ready, Douglas. 2019 "The Power of a Clear Leadership Narrative." *MIT Sloan Management Review*, September. https://sloanreview.mit.edu/article/the-power-of-a-clear-leadership-narrative/.

Roberts, Laura Morgan. 2005. "How to Play to Your Strengths." *Harvard Business Review*, January. https://hbr.org/2005/01/how-to-play-to-your-strengths.

Robson, David. 2023. "How to Take Control of Your Self-Narrative for a Better, Happier Life." *New Scientist*, January. www.newscientist.com/article/mg25634204-800-how-to-take-control-of-your-self-narrative-for-a-better-happier-life/.

Rosenberg, Marshall B., and Deepak Chopra. 2015. *Nonviolent Communication: A Language of Life: Life-Changing Tools for Healthy Relationships*. PuddleDancer Press.

Rousmaniere, Dana. 2015. "What Everyone Should Know About Managing Up." *Harvard Business Review*, January. https://hbr.org/2015/01/what-everyone-should-know-about-managing-up.

Rousseau, Denise M. June 1989. "Psychological and Implied Contracts in Organizations." *Employee Responsibilities and Rights Journal* 2 (2): 121–139. https://doi.org/10.1007/bf01384942.

Ryan, Richard M., and Edward L. Deci. January 2000. "Self-determination Theory and the Facilitation of Intrinsic Motivation, Social Development, and Well-being." *American Psychologis* 55 (1): 68–78. https://doi.org/10.1037/0003-066x.55.1.68.

Sakulku, Jaruwan, and James Alexander. October 2011. "The Impostor Phenomenon." *International Journal of Behavioral Science* 6 (1): 75–97. https://doi.org/10.14456/ijbs.2011.6.

Salovey, Peter, and John D. Mayer. March 1990. "Emotional Intelligence." *Imagination, Cognition and Personality* 9 (3): 185–211. https://doi.org/10.2190/dugg-p24e-52wk-6cdg.

Samide, Rosalie, and Maureen Ritchey. October 2020. "Reframing the Past: Role of Memory Processes in Emotion Regulation." *Cognitive Therapy and Research* 45 (5): 848–857. https://doi.org/10.1007/s10608-020-10166-5.

Schwarzer, Ralf, and Lisa Marie Warner. January 2012. "Perceived Self-Efficacy and Its Relationship to Resilience." In *Plenum Series on Human Exceptionality*, 139–150. https://doi.org/10.1007/978-1-4614-4939-3_10.

Seligman, Martin E.P. 2011. *Learned Optimism: How to Change Your Mind and Your Life*. Vintage.

Seligman, Martin E. P., Tracy A. Steen, Nansook Park, and Christopher Peterson. July 2005. "Positive Psychology Progress: Empirical Validation of Interventions." *American Psychologist/the American Psychologist* 60 (5): 410–421. https://doi.org/10.1037/0003-066x.60.5.410.

Senge, Peter M. (1990). *The Fifth Discipline: The Art and Practice of the Learning Organization*. New York, NY: Doubleday.

Sheppard, Blair, and Susannah Anfield. July 2020. "The Urgent Need for Sophisticated Leadership." *Strategy+Business*. www.strategy-business.com/article/The-urgent-need-for-sophisticated-leadership.

Sinek, Simon. 2011. *Start With Why: The Inspiring Million-Copy Bestseller That Will Help You Find Your Purpose*. Penguin UK.

Stelter, Susan. 2023. "Want to Advance in Your Career? Build Your Own Board of Directors." *Harvard Business Review*, July. https://hbr.org/2022/05/want-to-advance-in-your-career-build-your-own-board-of-directors.

Taylor, Bill. 2022. "Persuading Your Team to Embrace Change." *Harvard Business Review*, April. https://hbr.org/2022/04/persuading-your-team-to-embrace-change.

Tennant, Karie, Tammy J Toney Butler, and Ashley Long. 2023. "Active Listening." *Nih.gov*. *StatPearls Publishing*. www.ncbi.nlm.nih.gov/books/NBK442015/.

Thomas, Kenneth W., and Ralph H. Kilmann. 1974. "Thomas-Kilmann Conflict Mode Instrument." Data set. *PsycTESTS Dataset*, January. https://doi.org/10.1037/t02326-000.

Tichy, Noel M. 2009. *The Leadership Engine: How Winning Companies Build Leaders at E*. Harper Collins.

Tjan, Anthony K. 2014. "How Leaders Become Self-Aware." *Harvard Business Review*, July. https://hbr.org/2012/07/how-leaders-become-self-aware.

Tyrrell, Patrick, Seneca Harberger, Caroline Schoo, and Waquar Siddiqui. 2023. "Kubler-Ross Stages of Dying and Subsequent Models of Grief." *National Library of Medicine*. *StatPearls Publishing*. www.ncbi.nlm.nih.gov/books/NBK507885/.

Urrila, Laura Ilona. September 2022. "From Personal Wellbeing to Relationships: A Systematic Review on the Impact of Mindfulness Interventions and Practices on Leaders." *Human Resource Management Review* 32 (3): 100837. https://doi.org/10.1016/j.hrmr.2021.100837.

Ury, William. 2012. *The Power of a Positive No*. Hachette UK.

Van Woerkom, Marianne, Maria Christina Meyers, and Arnold B. Bakker. September 2022. "Considering Strengths Use in Organizations as a Multilevel Construct." *Human Resource Management Review* 32 (3): 100767. https://doi.org/10.1016/j.hrmr.2020.100767.

VIA Institute on Character. 2013. "Team Report." *VIA Institute on Character*. www.viacharacter.org/reports/the-via-team-profile-report.

Wepfer, Ariane G., Tammy D. Allen, Rebecca Brauchli, Gregor J. Jenny, and Georg F. Bauer. December 2017. "Work-Life Boundaries and Well-Being:

Does Work-to-Life Integration Impair Well-Being Through Lack of Recovery?" *Journal of Business and Psychology* 33 (6): 727–740. https://doi.org/10.1007/s10869-017-9520-y.

Woolley, Anita Williams, Christopher F. Chabris, Alex Pentland, Nada Hashmi, and Thomas W. Malone. October 2010. "Evidence for a Collective Intelligence Factor in the Performance of Human Groups." *Science* 330 (6004): 686–688. https://doi.org/10.1126/science.1193147.

Yahya, Azizul Halim, and Vidi Sukmayadi. December 2020. "A Review of Cognitive Dissonance Theory and Its Relevance to Current Social Issues." *Mimbar* 36(2): https://doi.org/10.29313/mimbar.v36i2.6652.

Zak, Paul J. 2013. *The Moral Molecule : The New Science of What Makes Us Good or Evil.* London: Corgi.

Zak, Paul J. February 2015. "Why Inspiring Stories Make Us React: The Neuroscience of Narrative." *Cerebrum: The Dana Forum on Brain Science*: 2. https://pubmed.ncbi.nlm.nih.gov/26034526.

Zenger, Jack and Joseph Folkman. 2016. "What Great Listeners Actually Do." *Harvard Business Review*, July. https://hbr.org/2016/07/what-great-listeners-actually-do.

About the Author

Dr. Belinda H. Y. Chiu focuses on individuals and organizations to cocreate healthier ecosystems and cultivate authenticity. Founder of Hummingbird research coaching consulting LLC, Belinda brings decades of experience in leadership development and training, executive coaching, consulting, public diplomacy, and higher education. An ICF-PCC, award-winning executive coach, she works across industries and has been featured at various forums such as the World Economic Forum. She serves as a leadership coach and program faculty for the Tuck School of Business and Executive Education programs and the Magnuson Center for Entrepreneurship at Dartmouth. A Search Inside Yourself Senior Certified Teacher and Teacher Trainer Faculty, she is an Inner MBA Faculty Member and Mind Gym Coach and Certification Trainer. Belinda helped to develop the Daniel Goleman Emotional Intelligence Coaching Certification Program and serves as faculty for the Embrace Change Coaching Certification Program. An International Liaison with the U.S. Department of State, Capacity Building Specialist with UNOPS, and the world's first certified consultant with CreativeID, she advises Music to Life to support musician social entrepreneurs and eiFOCUS to train coaches of female athletes.

Author of *The Mindful College Applicant* (Rowman & Littlefield), Belinda's writing has been featured in *Journal of Contemplative and Holistic Education, Mindful.org, Inside Higher Ed, UNESCO, Goleman EI, Key Step Media*, and *Thrive Global*, among other publications and academic journals. A certified yoga teacher, she is a Certified Forest Guide and a Valley Improv member. Belinda holds an AB from Dartmouth College, an MA from the Fletcher School of Law & Diplomacy, and an EdD from Columbia University. Her current research is on mycelial and organizational networks and shared humor as applied contemplation. She observes leadership behaviors in the forest with her pink-nosed puppy, Bandit.

Index